The Story of Jules Verne.

For Jeremy

[signature]

2010

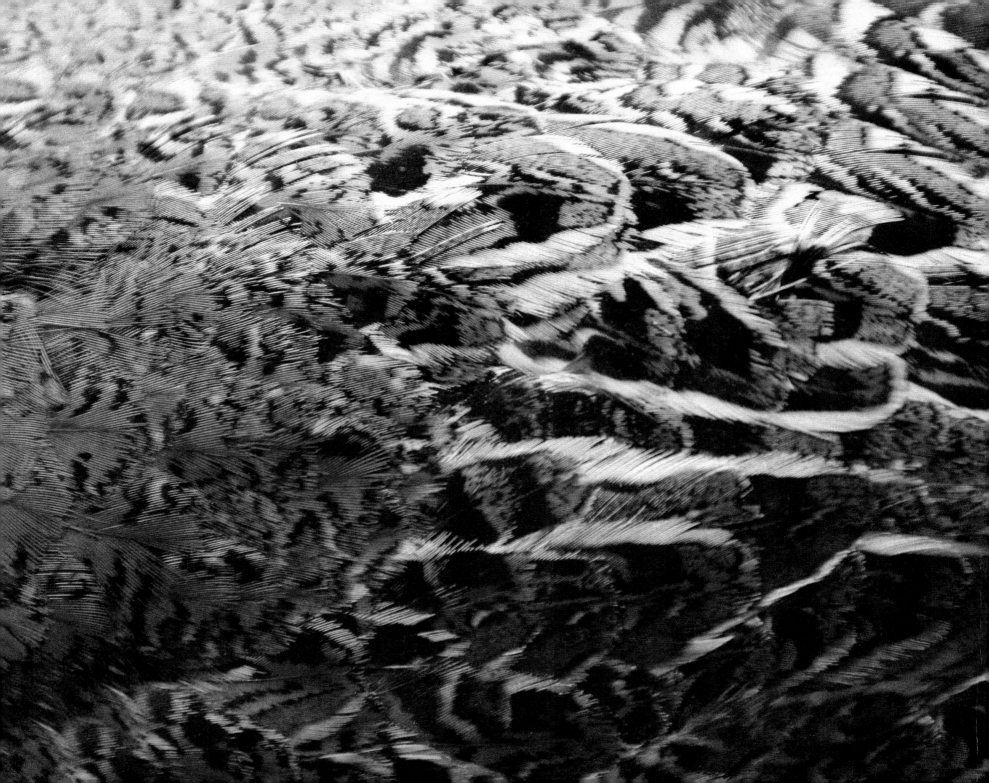

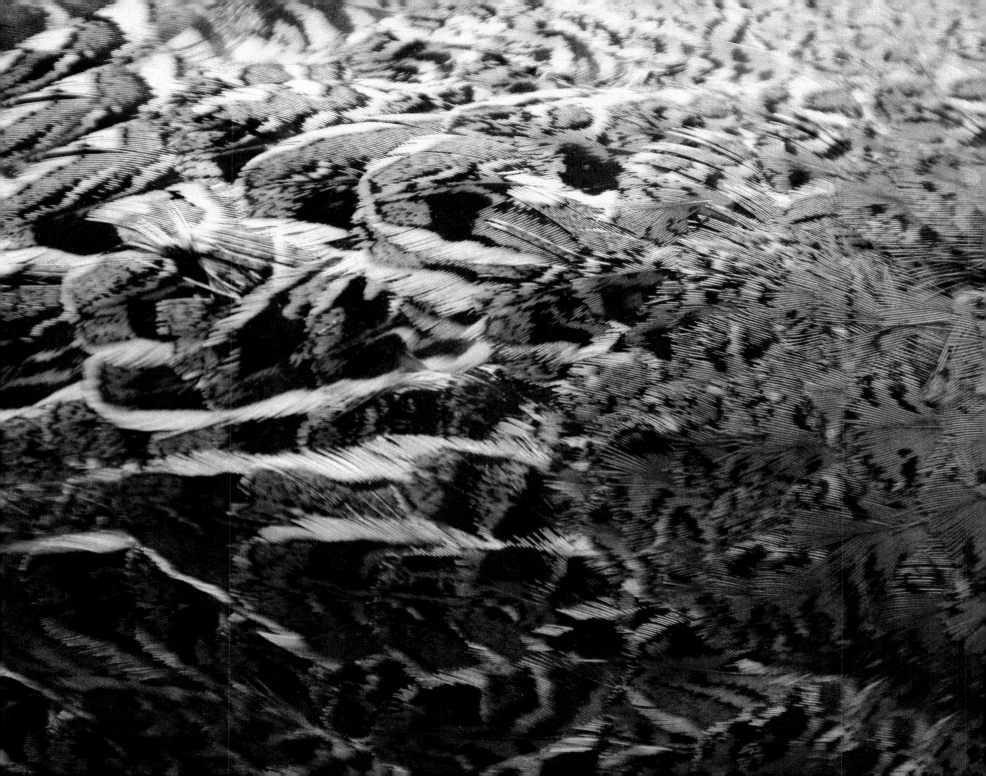

"Quitting Time Covey" 28x48

The Story of
JULES VERNE
A Watch Pocket Dog

"In the vernacular of the Southern Sportsman, the term "Bird Hunting" can refer to only one thing:
the Quest, preferably with the use of a fine double-barreled shotgun and a brace of well-trained pointing dogs,
of that elusive and noble Southern Gentleman himself, Mister Bob White Quail."

Story and Art by

WAYNE CALDWELL SIMMONS

Highlander Farm Press

ISBN-13: 978-0-615-28991-5

Produced with the invaluable assistance of Jim Huckabay, Jim Fritze, Kathy Sepulvado, Lel McCullough,
Paul Thornton, Weed Vail, Bubba Wood, Sandra Smith, Tammy Brinkley, Norbert Blei, John Taylor and Joel Ferrell

Cover Painting – from "Jules at the old Cottonwood log"

Published by Highlander Farm Press
200 Albert Avenue, Shreveport, LA 71105
Phone 1.318.861.3881

Printed in China
First Edition: 2009

Contents

"The Shaded Lane" 8x10

Prologue

When I was a boy we had a saying and because of our youthful ignorance we had occasion to use it a lot. It was an expression of such magnitude to us then that it stayed with me and to this day when invoked, continues to confuse and annoy people, particularly my wife. The expression or curious retort, to be more accurate, was coined by my old childhood friend, Paul Thornton, and it was called upon whenever anyone had the audacity to ask us a question that we didn't have a ready answer for — "How should I know; I'm not Jules Verne"! Hey, we were kids and those were powerful-sounding words to be sure, especially if you didn't know exactly what they meant. But smart-talking kids, short on information, occasionally need a device that baffles and bewilders — and stops the youthful inquisitor in his tracks (lest they find out the depth of your stupidity). Invariably, these surly interlopers had the strangest expressions on their faces. When we were very young they seemed to be thinking, "Who is Jules Verne, anyway?" And later on as we got older, "What in the hell does Jules Verne have to do with anything; I just want to know what such and such four-letter word means!" Whatever; however, the device seemed to work. We thought ourselves cool and our fragile little egos remained intact. Best of all, we had a hero in Jules Verne, the man with the plan, *The Man with All the Answers*.

To Gay, Marnie & Emily

"At the Barn" 16x20

Chapter 1

Jules

As natural as that first quivering puppy point, my early interest in the out of doors, and particularly the sport of bird hunting was instinctive. And like any kid who ultimately grows up to become a bird hunter, I wanted above all else to have my very own bird dog. From early on I looked forward to it. First I dreamed of owning a Setter; then a Pointer. Ultimately I got a Brittany spaniel. But that was 25 years later and, as I look back, he was a Brittany, I am sure, but at the time, he seemed one of questionable pedigree. At least, I questioned it then and to this day still experience twinges of guilt for those early feelings of doubt. How could a friend's bloodline affect the way you feel about him? And if it did, were you even worthy of that special friendship to begin with?

He entered our lives that day, a skinny foundling no one seemed to want. I can't even take credit for the find. My wife, Gay, rescued the one to two-year-old dog on her own after quietly watching him for weeks. The pitiful pup had been hanging out at the stable where she kept her horses, apparently living off cat food and the occasional luckless mouse. Extensive efforts had been made around the stable to locate the stray's owner, but to no avail. Finally, after overhearing the old codger who owned the place brag that he was going to shoot "the egg suckin' cur", she made up her mind. After all, hadn't her husband been obsessing about owning a bird dog for years?

While preparing to go home that late summer afternoon, Gay looked over at the scrawny little red and white dog sitting there all by himself in the doorway of the old barn.

He in turn watched her as he had done so many times before. Painstakingly, she packed up her tack that evening, her mind seemingly lost somewhere else — but not really. Occasionally throughout the ritual she'd look up and, with some difficulty, gaze down the long row of horse stalls toward the stable opening. The same incredibly depressing sight always met her eyes.

Grace (Gay's given name) Y. Simmons was not a casual thinker. Nor was she a casual doer. To her, motherhood and marriage, career and household responsibilities were all matters of extraordinary weight. Every move she made required deadly serious deliberation, usually followed by a good dose of self-doubt and further deliberation. A last minute inspection of the horses' water buckets that evening found them brimming. Good. She was a stickler for that one. Finally, confident that all was in order, she got into her car, started the engine and slowly began to drive away. Only this time the old Volvo wagon faltered a little at the turn, then came to a stop. As the car door swung open, the nice lady behind the wheel beckoned to the object of her discomfort. Twenty-one pounds of starving dog crawled up into that car and with a sigh, curled up on the floor and immediately drifted off to sleep.

Meanwhile, back at the agency, yours truly, probably fatigued from fending off yet another impatient media bill collector was carefully scanning the want ads in search of the ultimate bird-finding, canine treasure. For me, non-work related activities such as this often punctuated the normal workday and usually centered on some sort of hunting or fishing endeavor. These escape maneuvers were carried out periodically throughout the day — sometimes in epic proportions. No, they didn't call me "Mr. Duck" for nothin'! I'd earned that nickname fair and square. Normal people may rely on the occasional coffee break to ease the stress and monotony of the workday. But for me, no coffee was ever strong enough or its aroma fresh enough. My adrenaline rush came from a daily infusion of the Great Outdoors. And if I couldn't be there in person to enjoy it, then I'd be there in some other form. At this juncture in my life, bird dog shopping was my drug of choice. It had always been this way. For me, there was no escape like the great escape found only in the trusty woods.

Ah yes, the advertisement read, "For Sale: meticulously trained, impeccably bred Brittany spaniel male" *Perfect, no doubt, out of some elusive French lineage!* ... "$1000.00, firm." *Oops, next ad, please!* About that time there was a faint knock at the door. Opening it, I was surprised to see Gay standing there.

"I've got someone out in the car I want you to meet," she said with a sweet smile spreading across her face. "Oh, and who would that be?" I replied. "Why, Jules Verne," she taunted. "Who else could he possibly be?"

Jules didn't come with papers. He came with heartworms and an unappealing appreciation for garbage that was born of living on the street and in the woods. It was an odd predilection that followed him throughout his life. When I first laid eyes upon him I was shocked. I had never seen a hunting dog so small or pitiful, even a Brittany!

"What do ya think? You did say you wanted a Brittany spaniel!" she ventured.

"Gay, I want a quality dog, not some kind of scab dog!" *Oh, the Guilt!*

"Just look at those eyes. They bulge! A hunting dog's eyes do not protrude. They are deep-set in order to protect the animal in heavy cover. This dog is obviously no Brittany. In fact, I think he may instead be a rather large Pomeranian." *The Shame!*

It was then that I looked into those shiny monkey eyes of his and saw for the first time, just a glimpse of Jules Verne's inner soul. A kind of quiet dignity resided deep within those rheumy brown orbs and somehow, even under the direst of circumstances, he maintained a calm, trusting demeanor. I suspected then that for some lucky family at least, a very special relationship awaited.

"Maybe we'll give him a try after all," I conceded.

"Jules" 20x28

Chapter 2

Gay

Gay was born with a soft, sweet, loving heart and a sure sense of personal responsibility for all those she cared about. At two years of age she had snow white hair and a sturdy little square frame that propelled her all about. Gay was a wiggle worm. As a child her antics spurred hysterical laughter throughout the house whenever she went into one of her gyrations. While Gay-Gay, as she was called, was very young she lived with her mother and father and her sisters and brother in Shreveport, Louisiana. Even at that early age, she was known to be very generous with her siblings, frequently disappearing and then reappearing, a small gift held quietly behind her back. Her special offerings were the simple things of a child, like her very own little toothbrush (a favorite present), carefully wrapped in tissue and presented with a shy smile and a big hug. The process would be repeated often with a new recipient each time; but usually the same little toothbrush would be the chosen gift. Later on, after her parents divorced and the children were divided-up, she and her younger sister moved to Arkansas with their mother. There, Gay and "Little Ann" made it as best they could. Gay made sure that her sister was clothed and fed properly. She wasn't much of a cook at seven or eight but she did know how to prepare simple fare, like bacon and eggs and French toast. A lot of the time they wandered the countryside on their horses, mostly unsupervised. The little family lived out away from town on a dark, slow-moving creek where they had a tiny rowboat they named "turtle". After a big rain the girls would often board their craft and ride it downstream, dodging great boulders and low-hanging tree limbs that plunged ominously into the depths. This was

a turbulent period in their lives. But Gay made the most of things because she had a little sister who needed her and that was her nature.

Gay always loved animals. Horses and horseback riding would become her passion. This was something she shared with her mother, a sensitive woman of considerable intellect, who perhaps was better suited to the stage than motherhood. While living in Arkansas, Gay's pet menagerie included a variety of animals, both domestic and wild: baby squirrels and rabbits, dogs and cats, chickens, goats, horses and one extremely precocious piglet named Diana that sometimes lived under her bed. Once, Gay confided the story of a wild crow she had caught in her box trap. At first, Gay was very excited to have the crow, but as she transferred her captive into a holding cage the crow screamed and screamed at her, "Let me go, let me go! Can't you see, little girl, that I can not live like this!" So she released the crow. But the crow refused to leave. Instead, it took up residence in the trees surrounding her house and lived there for years with Gay feeding it horse feed every morning. Gay had no meanness in her. She was just a little towheaded woods creature surrounded by animals and a little sister who needed her.

When Gay was ten years old, she, Little Ann and her mother moved back to Shreveport. There the girls were reunited with their father, brother and sister and her grandparents who lived on the hill. This was both a joyous time for Gay and also a sad time. Several months before moving back to Louisiana, Gay began to notice a large red colored dog that emerged from the woods at dusk. The dog was obviously wild or, at least, extremely shy of humans. One evening, Gay was able to approach the feral dog and got within fifty feet of him before he became nervous. She found that if she crouched down low, never allowing her eyes to rise above his, he would allow her to crawl slowly towards him. Finally, as night closed

"Gin Rummy" 12x24

in, she laid her hands on him for the first time. He was huge, the color of whiskey, and covered from the tip of his broad nose down to his gaunt ribs with a hundred ugly fighting scars. Whether he came by his scars in the ring, for this was dog fighting country, will never be known. Or perhaps he was a genuine Arkansas "razorback hog dog"; that's a possibility, too. Anyway, Gay began bringing food to the big pit bull/hound cross every evening before dark and in time "Red Dog" became so enraptured with the little girl that he left the safety he had known and joined her at her home down from the woods.

The day they were to move, Gay's mother finally relented and gave her permission to take the wild dog back to Louisiana with them provided she could get him into the station wagon. Getting him into the car would prove to be the easy part. After a lot of coaxing, Gay finally lured Red Dog into the back seat beside her, but after closing the door behind him the dog suddenly went berserk and began throwing himself, time after time, against the closed windows of the car. Fearful that he would seriously hurt himself, Gay threw open the car door and Red Dog, like the crow, returned to the woods from whence he came. They stayed an extra day, with Gay pacing the wood line until night, hoping that he would return but it was not to be. I sometimes wonder if, for Gay, Jules Verne became that special red dog she had to leave behind in Arkansas as a girl.

8

Chapter 3
A Young Man in a Sportman's Paradise

As a young man in my second year in college, I remember, my father and I had a long conversation concerning what I wanted to do with my life. He was supportive of me and tried his best to be patient, but that was not always easy. I never was much of a student, as he'd gladly attest to if only he was here to tell. But I liked to read and I was a pretty fair hand when it came to art. So we decided then and there that I should pursue majors in English and Art. That sounded fine to me; I was probably dreaming of having a cold one with the boys about then anyway. Our conversations could get pretty intense. But exactly what does one do with such an odd, artsy sounding combination of studies? My father recommended strenuously that since I hunted and fished to the exclusion of *anything* else, that I write about my outdoor experiences and illustrate my own stories. That sounded way too good to be true and not the least bit lucrative to me, someone who had absolutely no clue as to anything. Instead, I decided to emulate one of my father's friends who was, to my way of thinking, a huge business success. He, being an advertising exec and by all accounts a very cool, "with it" kind of guy, became my role model. Naturally, at the time the world of advertising sounded a little more exciting to me, anyway. So that was the road I traveled.

It had been nearly fifteen years since that afternoon spent with my dad, discussing the future — my future. I had moved west by then and lived at the juncture of three extraordinarily diverse, outdoor sporting arenas. Here the temptations were great. To the north lay the hazy purple hills of Arkansas; and before them, literally at my feet, endless golden grain fields and all the amazing waterfowl opportunities a man could ask for. To the south lay the piney woods and verdant marshes and forbidding swamps of Louisiana, its fertile coastline literally teeming with fish and game. And to the west, the Hill Country and the vast plains of Texas, Oklahoma and Northern Mexico where the Bobwhite Quail is still King. Married now with two lovely daughters and all the responsibilities that go with that, I found myself in an odd predicament. The small once profitable advertising agency I owned and operated was no longer humming along famously, in fact, it was now struggling. Like a warm quilt, malaise began to envelop me.

Gay's timing couldn't have been better. Jules was exactly the tonic I needed and my spirits were buoyed from the start. Jules and I needed one another. And although his dire circumstances were undoubtedly greater than my own, the struggle I faced seemed considerable enough at the time. Ultimately my daunting problems at the office would work themselves out. Additional accounts were laid on and the media got paid. Things started clicking once again... just like the old grandfather's clock at the end of the hall.

"Grace" 16x20

Chapter 4
Trial by Feathers

I'd like to be able to say that there was no real trial phase for Jules — that from the beginning he was my dog and our relationship was so immediately unique and spontaneous that the very idea of a "try out" would have been, to this day, absolutely ludicrous. That would sound good; a noble sentiment I would be proud to espouse, but unfortunately that was not the elevated position I adopted. And because there are those about who know the truth, we'll have to go with the truth, no matter how distasteful it may sound. Fact is, *I was going to have a bird dog*, one way or another. And not just some generic mutt willing to follow me around in the woods, mind you, but one that exhibited real talent and matched my predatory zeal step for step. Jules Verne, *the Mystery Dog,* was going to have to possess significant pointing and retrieving instincts at the very least, if he wanted to stick around my house. As I look back though, even at this early stage in our relationship, I was keenly interested in his success.

So with the weekend coming up, Gay and I carefully planned Jules' "Trial by Feathers". First, I read a little book; I think it was entitled, "How to Train Your Bird Dog". That done, I dug around in my closet until I found an old training dummy I'd used with a previous hunting companion, a Labrador /Poodle cross we had been given by Gay's grandfather. The bright orange training apparatus I had used with "Grace" several years before seemed huge at the time considering Jules' tiny stature, but that's what I had. I even packed my camera. Finally I went out and bought a box of lively pen-raised quail. Every detail in place, I could hardly sleep the night before the big event. It was just like being a kid again. You may remember the feeling, the night before opening day?

There were three of them waiting for us at the diner the next morning, two of my old hunting buddies, the Rock and Jon Q=Petersen; the other's name and face I just can't recall. Rocky is a dentist and the only guy I ever knew who had cleanly dropped five birds on a covey rise (on two separate occasions, yet — and no, we don't ordinarily shoot doubles). Jon is just as competent with a shotgun, having once as a kid been offered a slot on the U.S. Junior Olympic Skeet Team.

They had heard about Jules and, true to form, were there for the show. Now if you knew these guys, you'd know right away that cutting me a little slack along the way wasn't an option. The insults began immediately. First came those from Rocky concerning the *suspicious* way I came by the dog. He stood there under the street light watching me, arms folded, his eyes narrowed down, that sly, sideways glance I had come to know, the eyebrow lifted for effect, assessing, reassessing. "Were there warrants for my arrest? Was this the way I intended to conduct my business in the future? Hmmm..." he wondered. "I read somewhere just the other day that your first name, 'Wayne', or was it 'Dwayne'; no matter... anyway, it is shared by almost 30% of the Nation's prison population. Now isn't that ironic?" Then came the inevitable questions concerning Jules' heritage, his stunted size, his poor coat and oozing sores. Finally, hearing enough, I feigned an exaggerated yawn and opened the car door. It was quite a drive up to our hunting lease in southwestern Arkansas, so Jules would probably welcome some exercise.

Immediately upon hitting the ground Jules began stalking a rather large dumpster. It was then I heard that strange snorkeling sound. It was the sound I'd become all too familiar with over the years: the sound of Jules making game. Slowly he circled the immense waste container, apparently intent on an early morning snack. Frankly, that was behavior I was hoping no one would notice, but Petersen, observant as always, espied the action immediately and gleefully remarked, "We've got our first point over there, Simmons. Your little 'watch pocket dog' (an obvious reference to Jules' pint-sized proportions) has that garbage can cold. Hurry, where's that camera? We'll preserve the moment with a snap shot!"

We arrived at the lease a little before daylight and, because it was teal season, the boys decided to give them a whirl before the "real entertainment" started. Now, I like duck hunting a lot; in fact, at the time of this story I had spent far more hours in a duck blind than I had walking behind a bird dog so, what the heck, I decided to join in. After making sure that Jules was safely squared away in the car, we headed for the duck blinds that were situated in adjacent rice fields. The hunting was only so-so that day but we did manage to down a few birds. Later we met up at the car and immediately got down to the real business at hand.

Jules' first assessment centered on his retrieving skills, which seemed perfectly logical at the time. Since I had no idea as to any of his abilities, I was somewhat at a loss as to what to do and when. For instance, how much training had he had, *if any*? Could he have possibly been someone's fully trained hunting dog? Or, more likely, was he a dog with no formal training whatsoever, but perhaps one with some good breeding to draw from? If so, I reasoned, he could still make a bird dog. And why not! As I recollect, Jules was rather casual about all this; he just sat there. When I first threw out the orange training dummy, Jules simply walked over to it, sniffed it, and walked off. I remember the gallery immediately went silent. Up until that moment, I was receiving all manner of helpful hints on what to do and in what order. Now their faces registered real concern. Embarrassment! After being sent out a half a dozen more times it was evident that Jules' strong suit was not going to be retrieving.

"Heck, I don't shoot all that well, anyway, heh, heh, heh... He won't need to retrieve!" I nervously quipped.

Looking around for a good place to wretch, I suddenly remembered the pile of blue-winged teal in the truck. Perhaps Jules was trained with a dead quail or some other animate object? Maybe he would respond more favorably to a small, tender teal? I threw the teal a few dozen times with essentially the same results. Once, on the very first toss he did walk over to the duck to sniff it before ambling over to a nearby tree to heist his leg. I was numb.

There wasn't a whole lot of conversation as we all loaded into the Rock's hunting van. No good humored jostling. No slicing repartee. And certainly no more enthusiastic dreams of what could be. How stupid! It was just beginning to sink in: Jules didn't have it. We drove down the dusty farm road in silence. Suddenly a small cloud of mourning doves exploded up ahead, then another, and another. We immediately piled out. Guns were quickly uncased and loaded. For my buddies, at least, the depressing past few minutes were momentarily forgotten. Doves were everywhere, and in the South they are considered game birds — not song birds. I struggled out of the vehicle and mumbled something about walking up ahead to check out the next milo field. What I really wanted to do was to get some fresh air and try to figure out what I was going to do about Jules. As disappointing as it had been to see Jules refuse to retrieve the hard plastic training dummy, the absolute indifference he showed to that fresh, still warm teal was what really concerned me. I didn't know much about training dogs but I did know this: desire is something you can't put into a hunting dog. All this, compounded by the realization that I had somehow already formed a bond with the dog had my head spinning.

After walking up the road a half a mile or so, I turned around and started back, still with no real sense of what I was

"Afternoon Pintails" 16x20

going to do. As I approached the boys, one thing was certain at least: they were having one whale of a shoot. "Petey", as I sometimes called Jon, was the first to notice me, but just barely; a dove was hurtling his way and, according to him, "If it flies it dies, hops it drops!" After taking the shot he turned and said with absolute disbelief, "Simmons, you're not going to believe this, but we've shot at least a dozen doves here and your dog, Jules, has retrieved every single one of 'em! It's the damnedest thing I've ever seen." About that time I saw Jules race across the field after a low flying bird Rocky had winged. Moments later he came out of the standing milo with the dove in his mouth and to my amazement, delivered it directly to Rocky's hand.

I learned a few things about Jules Verne that day: first, he did not retrieve dummies. Dummies were for dummies! What else could Jules have thought, watching grown men tossing about strange, garishly colored tumbling objects? Was this something humans did for their own amusement, some sort of Frisbee for the demented? Second, he didn't care to retrieve anything that you cast off. Apparently, if it wasn't good enough for you, then he didn't want any part of it. Makes sense! Not so curiously, he retrieved what you shot. Later on, I found that he also retrieved anything he managed to catch himself. He was very generous that way. And third, he did eventually do what any bird dog is ultimately expected to do; later that morning, Jules stylishly pointed each of the six pen raised birds we released, delivering for the most part all of them to hand after the shot (of course, with this glowing fool cheering him on all the way!).

Whether or not Jules had ever received formal training,

I'll never know. He may have been a natural bird dog. I guess that's possible. The big question for me, of course, will never be answered: would I have kept the little dog no one seemed to want, even if he had never pointed or retrieved a single bird? I hope so. At any rate, Jules Verne was definitely living up to his name.

Chapter 5
The Early Days

I recall a pale blue sky filled with small white fluffy clouds. The air was crisp and clean, freshly bathed by an old friend from the North, and the world smelled of freshly mowed hay. The tiny ten-acre patch where I stood was only a few blocks from our home. I had stumbled upon this wild oasis a year or two earlier while seeking the makings of a duck blind. The Johnson grass grew long and plentiful here and the young willows that bordered the small crescent-shaped lake were perfectly straight and leafy. Anyone who has built a duck blind from scratch knows the importance of finding just the right materials. Above all else, they must blend in with their wild surroundings; that is, if you expect to bag a few wary mallards for your trouble. And I always did. While gathering my materials that day I had been surprised to hear the soft, plaintive calls of bobwhite quail along the edge of the lake at dusk. At the time I didn't have a dog to pursue them so a mental note was all that was warranted, but fortunes sometimes change.

Now, standing beside me was my little hunting dog, Jules. This was to be our first-ever shared experience with wild quail and since this tiny parcel was located solidly within our city limits there would be no guns. Just as well, having wild birds that accessible to one's home was in itself an extraordinary stroke of luck for anyone interested in taking up bird dogs.

As I removed Jules' leash I noted the wind direction. It was blowing right up our skirts; steady out of the North — great for sailing but hardly ideal for us. For those unfamiliar with such things, it's always to the dog's advantage to have the wind

in his face when pursuing game. The air currents bring scent, allowing the dog to know when game is near and in which direction.

Because of the field's outlay and our position within it, the wind would not be in our favor that day. I released my dog. As Jules looked for room to quarter, he ran toward the lake and in so doing, passed through a small patch of beggar-lice and low, freshly cut briers that came up approximately mid-calf. Out of nowhere, Jules countenance changed as he abruptly turned like a fishhook — mid-air — and froze. Jules had failed to smell his quarry in time, overrunning the covey. I wonder who was most surprised, the birds or Jules! Now plopped right there amongst them, with one back foot still raised, as if careful not to step on anyone, he stood there frozen. Because of the speed of his progression and the abruptness of the statue-like point, he set them... meaning, when he froze; they froze — eye to eye. From then on it would be a standoff, as to who would make the next

move. That's how it works. A thousand years ago early hunters would have approached such a pointed dog and simply cast a large net over both dog and prey. Now, as I approached from the rear, I had neither net nor gun, but I was fully engaged all the same. I noticed Jules' exaggerated U-shaped point. It was very dramatic, and the incredulous look in his eyes was sort of frantic. They seemed to say, "Look here..." gesturing to a spot somewhere underneath his tucked rump. My eyes were glued on that exact spot as I walked in, but frankly, I could see nothing out of the ordinary, just weeds.

A skilled magician could not have accomplished his slight of hand any better. Right before my eyes, the knot of twisted stems, branches and briers slowly dissolved into a moving, swirling, living thing... or things. Like a horde of hornets, the covey exploded literally underneath the dog filling the sky with a dozen flapping, flailing projectiles now hurtling toward the thick cover along the lakeshore. Oh, how I praised him afterwards, while stroking his noble little head and quivering shoulders. "Wow, that was quite an opening performance," I thought to myself. "Maybe he'll do it again!" And he did, time after time that afternoon and on each progressive occasion it was as if Jules was trying to outperform his last maneuver. Like a scrawny little wood sprite he launched into a fantastic woodland virtuoso. Jules seemed to swirl and pivot all around the ten acre patch, occasionally freezing with only his eyes in motion, looking to me, his ultimate fan; searching for that special approval only I could provide. Three separate coveys fell to Jules' rock-solid points that afternoon and a dozen more flustered singles and pairs, too, that nervously flushed, then sailed away into the wind. I would have never guessed that such a small bit of habitat could have supported that many birds, but it did. And what a valuable training ground it would become.

In the weeks that followed, Jules and I wandered over considerable Arkansas and Louisiana real estate. Quail weren't nearly as plentiful out in the wild as they had been closer to home in our little urban honey hole, but we managed to bag a few. These were very special times. I remember Jules' first water retrieve when I dropped a fat bobwhite into a farm pond. Jules had absolutely no fear or opposition to water, a real plus.

During the early duck season when it was still warm, Jules and I would often share a makeshift blind out on the Red. As long as the river was low, we were okay out on the sand bars, scrunched-up tight against some sort of flotsam, making like a log. Jules would retrieve anything. When things were slow he'd bring me an occasional rabbit or squirrel, whatever he managed to catch. How do you discourage that kind of generosity even if the behavior is generally frowned upon? Once, while hunting alongside a Louisiana bayou, Jules caught and killed a medium-sized nutria. Nutria can be dangerous to dogs due to their formidable, beaver-like front teeth. These large South American rodents have, over time, become established throughout the southern United States and are trapped for their fur. I recall Jules brought the nutria to me proudly and I did reluctantly accept his gift, not really knowing what to do with it, but pleased that he was willing to share. We had hardly gone another hundred yards when, to my amazement, I witnessed him dragging in another nutria; this one still alive and snapping, and so outsized (perhaps twenty-five pounds), that Jules was actually having to drag it to me backwards!

Since Jules' "Trial by Feathers," Gay and I and our children, Marnie and Emily, had been spending our evenings with him, getting better acquainted. Like most fellows my age, I was brought up on "Lassie" and the exploits of "Rin, Tin, Tin" and although Jules never actually saved my life as his television counterparts had done for their masters, he was still quite fond of me, I am sure. In fact, rarely did he ever leave my side. Whenever a door separated us, I immediately heard a long, exaggerated inhalation from underneath the door, his breathing. At times, this could be a little disconcerting.

Besides tracking my every move around the house, Jules' favorite evening pastime was watching "mouse-a-vision", or so our children named it. As with most American families, television played a significant role in our everyday family life.

"Gay and Gin" 32x48

Nightly entertainment for Jules though was a little different. Mouse-a-vision involved a large aquarium located in our den that housed my daughter's pet mouse. Jules would sit there in front of the mouse for hours; head tilted, drooling, in some sort of Pavlovian trance. While the entertainment ran through his nightly wheel exercises, "Kitty Amin", our huge, striped tom cat and his brother "Agent Orange", would take up the other side of the tank. They too, shared Jules' fascination with mouse-a-vision; also drooling, offering the same brain-dead, trance-like state. It must have been an odd sight: all the Simmons' and their varied nightly viewing rituals; man and beast alike, transfixed… and not a creature was stirring except one rather robust, manic-mouse giving that treadmill hell. So welcome to middle-America, folks! If ever you wondered what the neighbors were up to, now you know.

Although Gay was solidly behind me on most all things concerning Jules, it's only fair to say that she was sometimes less than enthusiastic when it came to my hunting. Let's face it: she had been burned. My involvement in outdoor activities, hunting only being one, bordered on legend. You'd immediately know that if ever you scanned one of our family photo albums. Example: here we have photos of my dear Gay, up to her elbows in putting on yet another one of our children's birthday parties — and then we have a few snapshots of dear old Dad, standing around amongst the little party goers in his bird hunting boots and britches, forever checking his watch, but trying to remain useful and at the same time not look too conspicuous. Obviously, Gay lived in the trenches with the kids while I reconnoitered and battled

a hostile bird crop out on the western front.

Jules was fitting in just fine. But for Gay and me there were still a couple of issues that deeply concerned us both. Although efforts had been made in the beginning to locate Jules' rightful owner (all to no avail), we were worried that someday someone would appear out of nowhere to claim him. There was always the off-chance that Jules would be recognized. What then? Just how much would we be willing to pay? Being the proactive paranoiac that I was, and still am, I frantically bootlegged him around town for years on the floorboards of my car, as if he was some sort of reclusive Hollywood celeb. *Oh, the embarrassment!*

Legitimacy issue resolved somewhat, our next hurdle was Jules' health. He had put on a little weight since joining us and he was looking a lot better, but after a thorough examination, our veterinarian had some bad news. Jules was infected with heartworms and we were assured that the required 90-day treatment would be both hard on the dog and expensive for us. Essentially, the regimen was this: the patient would be poisoned little by little, with each deadly dose made progressively stronger until finally, hopefully, only the healthy dog remained and the worms did not. Theoretically, the parasites would die where they lived, within the chambers and the muscle of the heart itself. We understood that after death these slimy little intruders would slowly disintegrate (the most dangerous phase in the treatment) and ultimately be expelled from their host, once and for all, never to return. We thought.

"Brothers" 16x20

Chapter 6

A Boy and His Hunter's Heart

I remember my father standing at the door of my closet hanging up my clothes. As he straightened out my trousers on a clothes hanger, something fell from one of the pockets and onto the floor. My father reached down and picked up the object and examined it. It was a small, sweet smelling sachet bag. He then asked me where I had gotten it and I told him. I was five years old. Our family had been shopping that afternoon at a department store and while standing there before a display of these curious, pleasant smelling cloth bags I had absent-mindedly placed one in my pocket, thinking them free. I can only assume this to be true, although it is possible that I consciously stole the object. I just can't remember. Anyway, my father wasn't taking any chances. He looked at me in horror and asked, "Did you pay for this?" "No, I don't have any money," was my reply, *I guess*. My father was pretty upset; you'd have thought I had just knocked over an armored car. He lectured me for an hour on the perils of thievery.

The next morning at school my teacher went to the door of the kindergarten class and began talking to someone outside. After a moment, she returned to the class and beckoned for me to come forward. My father was there to get me. He didn't say much as he drove me back to the department store where we'd been the day before. Dad took me directly up to the Lady's Department where he found the "sachet bag display" and the woman who ran that part of the store. He turned to me and said with his deep, intimidating voice, "Now I want you to go over to that lady and tell her what you've done. Then I want you to return this (handing me the small sachet bag), and I want you to apologize and say that it will never happen again.

And I did, with tears streaming down my face. Now whether I purposefully stole the little bag of crushed flowers I really can't say. But because of this early humiliation, any idea of a life of crime was forever thwarted. End of story.

My father raised me right. And since hunting was an all-consuming preoccupation of mine, gun safety and hunting ethics were issues of primary concern to him. According to my father, anyone involved in blood sport was solemnly required to show the proper respect, both for the animals pursued and the laws protecting them.

Once while quail hunting with my father and a friend of his, the dogs began flash pointing then moving ahead to reset. The birds were running ahead of the dogs, as they'll often do, in an attempt to elude them. I was standing off to the side, really sort of out of the action I thought, when the little covey

"A Boy and His Pony" 30x36

ran clear of cover and directly onto a dim little cow path and then away from me. I threw up my little 410 L.C. Smith double and fired one shot. When the dust cleared, three bobwhites lay flopping on the path. I was pretty proud of myself because there's nothing better than fried quail covered with rich brown gravy, mashed potatoes, English peas and hot biscuits. But my dad was not impressed. He came over, placing his big hand on my shoulder, and said quietly, "Buck (as he sometimes called me), you are young and don't know any better, but we don't shoot these little country gentlemen on the ground. That's just not a sporting proposition for 'Old Bob'; in fact, your grandfather once told me in a situation very much like this one, that there were only two things he'd whup me over — hitting girls and shooting birds on the ground."

Although my father worked very hard and had to spend a great deal of time away from home he always managed to find occasion to take me hunting and fishing. His interest in the sport of hunting paled in comparison to mine, but that never slowed his determination in getting me into the woods. We duck and goose hunted regularly, as we did bird hunting. We even had a few bird dogs. And every year we went to Mississippi where we hunted Whitetail deer, plantation style: using hounds, horses and standers.

One of my big regrets growing up was a missed opportunity to go bear hunting in the Smokey Mountains with my father and some acquaintances of his from Newport, Tennessee. These old fellows had pursued black bear and wild boar for generations. They were real mountain men who hunted with ferocious bear dogs, mostly Plott hounds and a few black and tans. Due to the mountainous terrain we would encounter, it would be an extremely arduous affair, to say the least, especially for a twelve-year-old but I was eager for the challenge. The dates were set, the trip planned and since it was to be my first bear, it was agreed that I would shoot the first one during our five-day hunt. Sadly for me, word got out and my school teacher stepped in and nixed the hunt a couple of days before we were to leave. Later, we heard that our party had treed and killed a huge four hundred pound male the second day.

Most of the time growing up we lived in Nashville, Tennessee which was only about three hours from my father's hometown of Paris. For as long as I can remember we had a membership in a small waterfowl hunting club there on the edge of the Big Sandy Federal Wildlife Refuge on Kentucky Lake. I have fond memories of our time spent in Paris. I remember the big two story red brick home where my father lived as a boy and the circular goldfish pond in the garden where I, as a child, had discovered fishing. Whenever I encounter the acrid smell of coal smoke, I am immediately carried back to this pretty little town where coal was used to warm its homes in winter. As a kid I prowled its frigid streets

"Jumpin' Jack" 11x16

during the Christmas holidays, visiting family and friends. To me, Paris was always home.

Back in those days we hunted from daylight till dark. Once, my father left me alone in our goose pit while he went back to town for sandwiches. I fell asleep on the bench while he was gone and I was suddenly awakened by a cacophony of approaching Canada goose calls. As I peeked over the outer edge of my blind I saw three Giant Honkers approaching our decoy spread. Just as they came over me I threw up my 3-inch magnum and fired twice, killing two of them. This was quite an occasion for me because although I had several hunting seasons under my belt, I had never officially bagged a Canada goose before and there I was with a double (the legal limit), and with only two shots. My surprise turned to absolute jubilation when I discovered that my Dad had witnessed the whole thing while approaching thirty yards down the fence line. I remember he was clapping, hooting and hollering for all he was worth.

At the age of thirteen my father allowed me to go hunting unsupervised with my friends for the first time. I wouldn't say that this rite of passage was particularly rushed, since I recall many hunts that I missed due to my youth and lack of experience. For years the rudiments of gun safety and hunting ethics were pounded into my head and also the heads of all my little friends who joined my Dad and me in the field. My best friend, Paul Thornton, certainly was never exempt from my father's watchful eye.

The day my father told me that I was ready to go it alone, was the day he told me that I should always remember one thing when afield: "No one is immune from a hunting accident, no matter how careful, well-schooled or well-intentioned he may be. The shot once fired, cannot be called back. Remember it, Buck."

Chapter 7
Living the Dream

They say every bird hunter has the opportunity to own at least one truly outstanding gun dog at some point in his life. Jules was that special dog for me. Sure, to some he was just another "meat dog," but for this lucky nimrod, no pointing dog ever exhibited more desire in his quest for game or looked more stylish, once he'd found it. He may not have been the finest bird dog that ever lived. Even I have hunted with some that were in many ways superior. They just happened to belong to someone else (perhaps that hunter's special "once in a lifetime dog"). No matter; I wouldn't have traded Jules for the lot of 'em! Jules suited me. And, although he possessed all the characteristics you'd associate with a top-notch bird dog; nose, style, endurance, and desire, it was, I think, his diminutive size that enthralled and exhilarated me most. Everyone loves the underdog, the runt that grows up to be the strongest, the best, the leader of the pack. At his heaviest, Jules weighed barely thirty-two pounds. So small was he in fact that "he" was usually referred to as "she". For me, there was something magical in seeing a gun dog of Jules' humble stature and delicate features competing favorably with dogs much larger and stronger than he was. Let's face it: my heart swelled with pride on these occasions.

Once, out in West Texas near Albany, I experienced one of these priceless happenings. It was especially meaningful to me then in that it was the first of many such events Jules and I would share. But first, there's a key player in the scenario who needs to be introduced. His name was Blume Johnson. Blume was the father of one of my friends, John Johnson, and why he took me under his wing at that time I can't say. But like-minded people have a tendency to gravitate toward one another. And in bird hunting, at least, differences in age, social strata, financial stroke and education don't even figure in. Our bond was a common love of birds and the dogs that pursue them.

We met one day on a piece of ground Blume ran cattle on. I handled their company's advertising, so John and I worked together frequently. John and I were there to scout out an old cyprus swamp that we planned to hunt the following morning, which just so happened to be opening day of duck season. I hadn't as yet had an opportunity to tell John about a conversation that I had had the evening before with our mutual friends: Rocky and Jon Petersen. Sadly (for them), they were without a place to hunt on "the Opener" and they, of course, wanted me to pave the way for them to join us. Sure, why not! Actually, this sort of thing would hardly faze John Johnson. He was pretty laid-back; a golfer really, who had little interest in hunting. John was involved in this caper strictly to accommodate my obsession.

No sooner had we arrived at the cyprus swamp where we

"The Usurper" 32x48

planned to hunt, than John apologized that he had forgotten about an important golf tournament scheduled for that weekend and that he wouldn't be able to hunt with me the following morning. So Blume volunteered to show me around, and later that evening, take me home. Naturally, I let John off the hook. This really wasn't his forte, anyway.

Blume and I spent the rest of the afternoon touring his ranch. Life had been good to Blume. Although the sixty odd year-old oilman had little use for idle chatter, he was friendly enough. He had spent most of his life working hard in the oil fields. He was intelligent and well educated: a tough old gent who'd earned the respect of everyone around him. The oil boom was in full swing then, and Blume and his boys, astute businessmen, had picked just the right moment to secure an outside investor and to sell their drilling company, of course, making millions in the process. Unfortunately for their buyer and other speculators like them, boom would soon turn to bust. But Blume and his sons were well beyond all that.

About sundown we started home. I look back now and still shake my head in disbelief because what happened next was really kind of funny although extremely stressful and embarrassing for me at the time. As I recall, Blume was driving, with me in the passenger seat and Jules sitting there in the middle between us. Somewhere along the way it started raining. And, Man, did it rain. It was about that time that Blume confided that the finger of land I'd be hunting on in the morning was not actually his, although he had leased it to run his cattle on.

"If you happen to run into anyone back there tomorrow morning while you're hunting..." Blume cautioned, "...Well, just tell 'em that you're my son. I think that would be the best way to handle it. The landowner's kind of touchy, but if you tell him you're my son, I think he'll be alright with that."

"Okay..." (*Pops?*) I thought.

Until that very moment I had forgotten totally about Rocky and Jon Petersen and my earlier commitment to them. I wished then that I hadn't been so generous with John's hospitality, or rather now, *Blume's hospitality*.

Oh, I didn't like this. The more I thought about it, the more anxious I became. Meanwhile Jules had curled up beside me and had fallen asleep. How peaceful he looked.

After carefully considering all my options, it became obvious that I was going to have to broach the subject with Blume, whom I hardly even knew. Really, I'm not generally the pushy type. At least I hope I'm not, especially in a situation that could be construed as self-serving. But there I was nonetheless, wailing away on a perfectly fine, budding friendship — just pushy as hell!

"Gosh, it's hot in this car!" I blurted. Blume seemed startled.

"I don't think so? But I can turn on the air conditioner for you."

"Thanks," I mumbled, noticing that droplets of moisture were forming all over my forehead. My inner discomfort was such that I was sweating profusely, so much so that my side of the windshield was all fogged up. I'm creating a safety hazard, I thought! Furiously I mopped away at the condensation with my jacket. "Blume, I've got a little problem."

"Oh, what's that?"

"Well, you see... a friend of mine asked if he could join us in the morning ... uhh, uhh, in order to go hunting with me." I stammered like an idiot.

"Well, we can work that out. Really it would probably be safer for you to have someone with you, but please tell your friend that if anyone asks what you two are doing back there, that you are both my sons... and that you do have permission to be there. That landowner can be a real S.O.B."

"Sure, Blume — Thanks." Silence. By then, perspiration

was running down my face and my shirt was wringing wet and, no matter how hard or fast I rubbed the windshield with my jacket, the cloud on my side of the car remained.

"Something must be wrong with your vent; I can hardly see out your side of the windshield." he said with growing concern.

I looked down — the little bastard beside me was sleeping like a baby! How I wished that I could switch places with Jules.

We were on my street by then, thank goodness, and if given a choice, I would have gladly leapt from that moving vehicle rather than say what I was about to say.

"Blume, there's one more thing I need to ask you about..."
"Yes."

"I hate to put you in this position, but I have another friend who doesn't have anywhere to hunt tomorrow, either. Do you suppose it would be all right if he joined us in the morning?"

"You mean, as my third son?" Blume asked incredulously. Did I detect just a trace of ire in his voice? I ignored it.

"Yes, Blume, would that be possible?"

"Well, yes, I suppose so, actually I do have three sons, men your age, and I don't suppose the landowner knows any of them. Now that would be a little awkward." As I exited the vehicle, Blume's parting words sounded sort of pitiful.

"Now Wayne, let's get our story straight. I've got three sons — you and two other guys I've never met — and who may or may not look anything like me, or you, right?"

"Right!"

"And, you're not going into that house and invite any other people between now and daylight, are you?" "Oh, no sir, that's one thing you don't have to worry about."

As Blume drove away I could see that he was frantically wiping off the inside of the windshield, *his side* now as well as my own. I marveled at his warmth and capacity for human kindness. I felt like family.

I'm happy to report that our duck shoot the next morning went off without a hitch, meaning we didn't have any irate landlords come crashing through our decoys; just empty skies and no ducks! I might as well have been golfing. And although I wasted little time letting my hunting buddies know just how far I'd gone out on a limb for 'em the evening before, they naturally ignored it all and instead complained bitterly all morning about how I had led them on yet another wild goose chase.

Apparently Blume was not one to hold grudges, because two weeks later we were driving through Fort Worth with his dog trainer on our way to his bird lease further to the west. As we drove over a railway overpass downtown Blume casually remarked that during the Great Depression fifty years before, he had entered Fort Worth as a hobo, riding a slow freight all the way downtown. I think it gave him pleasure to reflect on those early days. If the young man who rode the rails all those years before could have looked into the future that day and seen himself, a successful businessman, he would have been pleasantly surprised and no doubt, a little relieved. Blume was an admirable guy who not only survived a difficult time in American history but came away a stronger more resilient individual.

Remember earlier, before I diverged, when I referred to a "landmark event" where Jules' performance in the field made my heart swell with pride? This was the occasion and it happened the first morning of our hunt. Mental images that were created then still exist in my brain today. There's no denying it; the event captured my imagination. So beautiful was it to my eyes, that it begged to be captured on canvas or, at least, in print.

It was a heavy, foggy morning, fairly dripping with dew (perfect scenting conditions, we thought). But although quail were in abundance here on Blume's lease, we were not having much success. The birds were hanging tight, still on the roost even at nine-thirty in the morning.

"West Texas Pointers" 24x30

As almost everyone knows, bobwhite quail roost on the ground, sitting shoulder to shoulder, tail to tail, in a tight little circle. All eyes are protectively positioned to look out in every possible direction. While on the roost, the birds' scent is held in to some degree by their interlocking tails and wings, thus affording them that much more protection from predators. It's an inhospitable world for Mr. Bobwhite. He is always vulnerable, and predators abound. On the ground, bobcats, foxes, feral cats and coyotes all prey on the tasty little birds, as do hawks and falcons in the sky. Typically, quail find favorable roosting areas in overgrown fields and in open CRP* acreage. Moderate to heavy ground cover is essential, and overhead obstructions are avoided. Hawks can perch in trees. When faced with impending danger, the little feathered bombshells will literally explode through the cover, creating a thunderous, deafening blast that often stupefies their adversary, thus allowing them valuable time to make good their escape.

Our party had been hunting for well over an hour and in desperation, my host started putting down more and more dogs. Finally, after releasing his fourth bird dog, Blume invited me in his characteristic laconic style to put "her" down (of course, referring to Jules).

Blume had never hunted with Jules before and I think he was a little skeptical of my little "watch pocket dog". Heck, at the time I hadn't hunted with Jules all that many times myself, so I was a little uneasy. I knew he had a weakness for rabbits — strictly a no-no in this setting; we were conscientiously working on that aspect of his training at home, but the power of the bunny must be tremendous. So with a silent prayer I released my dog, thinking, "Just maybe the hippity-hops are burrowed in deep like the quail are today...

* Conservation Reserve Program, a Federal farm subsidy/conservation program
  that encourages the creation of wildlife habitat

I hope. I hope. I hope."

Jules was in some pretty fancy company, all right. Running alongside him that day were two solid, wide-ranging Pointers: a liver and white Rip Rap dog and a slippery lemon Elhew bitch Blume swore by. Rounding out the field were his pride and joy, a breath-taking English setter he called Babe and another Brittany, one almost twice the size of my little Jules.

We hadn't gone far, perhaps only a few hundred yards when Jules dropped out of sight. Blume's highly esteemed dog trainer/handler was the first to locate him. "Your dog is down* over here," Joe cryptically announced, his condescension purposefully unmasked, "Maybe he's got a rabbit!"

"Oh boy; now they're reading my mind," I thought to myself.

As I topped the little rise that stretched before us, a beautiful composition began to unfold. Jules hung rock solid on the far side of a naked wash, his back foot still raised as if frozen in mid-stride, his head faced forward while his eyes were locked in hard to the left. Somewhere under that big cottonwood log and brush top breathed game — *A bunny perhaps!* One by one, each of the other dogs arrived: first, the Setter with her beautiful, white flowing flag, then the cat walking Brittany, and finally, the wide running Pointers with their twelve-o'clock high tails. Each, honoring Jules' find, fell into his own exquisite cast iron point, until finally the painting was complete. Slowly we walked in amongst them. At the last possible moment, Blume turned to me, and with a little smile, kicked the old cottonwood log. The explosion was startling even for hunters who'd been there many, many times before. It seemed like every quail in West Texas was huddled up under that log.

* Pointing game

"Jules at the Old Cottonwood Log" 30x48

Chapter 8

Adventures on the Border

Every dog has his day. Obviously, Jules had his moments, too, and although it's a lot of fun writing about stylish points and grand retrieves, the truth is Jules could occasionally be "less than perfect" — particularly when teamed up with some other wayward mutt. One inauspicious occasion readily stands out.

It occurred a little over a year after Jules came aboard; for me, it was a real character-building experience. Once again we were in Texas, where many of our escapades took place. I was the guest of my brother in law, Dick McDougall, a member of a wonderful bird lease in Carrizo Springs, a little sleepy village down near the Mexican border. Dick knew all about Jules. I'd literally worn him out with glowing reports. Still, Dick had never had the pleasure of hunting with my new dog.

You see, my first hunting season with Jules was spent for the most part on the den couch, sharing milk shakes and watching television. Poor little Jules' difficult 3-month long heart worm treatment called for an exercise-free lifestyle (lest a dissolving worm particle break loose and become terminally lodged in his lungs or heart). So our first bird season was a short one. Jules did fine though, always pointing and retrieving his share of wild birds.

In any event, Dick was kind enough to invite us down to the San Pedro Ranch for the opening weekend of quail season. What an opportunity! With us that weekend, was Jules' new brace mate, a beautiful, fat and fine Brittany bitch I had bought just days before. I was ecstatic, living the dream at last! I had never hunted with "Spanky" (that name should have told me something), but I was salivating at the prospect. Visions of Jules and Spanky windshield wiping across the South Texas landscape lulled me to sleep the night before our foray south. Vividly I recounted the dog trader's (*traitor?*) enthusiastic words:

"She'll do it all... Points...Backs... and Retrieves!" All this for just three hundred dollars? *Why, I should be ashamed.*

In early November, South Texas is hot. The bobwhite quail were whistling in the cactus; we could see them darting in and out as we came rolling down the dirt runway at the edge of the lease. It was late in the afternoon and we were tired, having flown in direct from our home in Shreveport, Louisiana. Dick's an airplane pilot and at the time worked for an aviation company based in Shreveport.

After parking the twin-engine Cessna, we quickly unloaded our gear and started for the compound. Immediately we came upon an immense rattlesnake lying on the pure white caliche road, soaking up the last of the sun's warmth. It's interesting how flat they get, pressing and spreading for maximum surface contact. Rattlesnakes are a natural hazard for bird hunters and bird dogs alike in the South and the West. Thankfully, this was the only one we saw on this particular trip.

The next morning, Dick and I, and a mutual friend, Blake Boyd, hunted together on a vast mesquite-dotted pasture. Jules hadn't been on birds since the previous hunting season but I wasn't worried. He had already proven himself admirably. And although Spanky was something of a question mark, I had confidence in her, all the same. Proudly I took each dog from its box; admiring and stroking them individually — in fact, asking my comrades what they thought about their size and color, their conformation. They were polite.

One by one I released my darlings, unaware of the

"Cantina Dogs" 30x48

conspiracy they plotted. Now, anybody that says Brittany spaniels can't cover ground did not witness what we witnessed that morning. True to my earlier euphoric dreams, they covered the South Texas landscape all right — but not like a windshield wiper, more like a scythe. Their attack was direct: they ran quickly like uncontrollable, deranged Huns from Covey A, to Covey B, to Covey C, and on — pointing nothing, but flushing everything — until the entire pasture had been emptied of every living creature. All of this, in what seemed to be mere seconds! I remember turning to my colleagues as they boarded their escape vehicle, "You'll tell your children and your grandchildren about this day. Where are you going?" I yelled as they drove away.

Later that afternoon, no amount of cajoling, excuses or apologies would heal the rift. I told my buddies that after separating the pair, Jules was once again his old self: finding, then pointing and holding every bird he came across. I told them that he had, in fact, seemed almost remorseful about his earlier behavior. They rolled their eyes at this. I tried to engage them further. I told them about a chance meeting I had had with an old acquaintance of theirs, a Mr. W.J. Lester who guided and trained dogs next door at the Crystal Oil Company hunting lease. Dick then informed me that Blake was in negotiations with Lester on a fine pair of raw-boned pointers (ones "suitably trained", of course) and, furthermore, we were all invited to their camp for supper. "Please don't embarrass us," were his parting words.

I neglected to tell my companions the whole story — how I had confessed to Lester about the disappointing morning we'd had, and how my new "trained Brittany" had used her witchy female ways in an attempt to take over Jules' mind. Lester was very understanding, having occasionally dealt with devious females and unscrupulous bird dog traders in the past himself. Fastening his eyes on Spanky for the first time, there came a

curious spark of recognition. "Son, I know that dog..." Lester chortled, "And one thing sure, she ain't broke!" Lester was obviously a big fan of understatement. "You're gonna have to come down hard on that little gal. That's the only way you're gonna break her. But don't worry, Son, she's old enough to take a little whoopin'. And by the way, that old boy you bought her from — I know him, too. Son, he don't have a heart — all he's got is a thumpin' gizzard, right here!" Lester said, slapping his chest. "Next time you want a trained bird dog, you come see old W.J. Lester."

About that time, Jules happened to lock up on a nice covey on the opposing hillside and Lester commented on "the little dog's keen nose and stylish point". With that said, he abruptly drove off in a cloud, heading over to his own lease. Lester's observations concerning Jules' birdy nature were the kind of encouraging words my shattered psyche needed. So with newfound exuberance, I continued my work.

For several hours I worked with Spanky on wild birds. She was obstinate at first, refusing to hold point, busting every covey and single bird she came across. But there's never been a better place to train a green dog than South Texas, one of the last real strongholds for bobwhite quail in America. Amazingly, on her fourth covey, Spanky actually held the point! Now that was encouraging. Although she displayed an incredible array of bad habits that morning, Spanky was beginning to come around. It would be later, months later, and after a lot of hard work that Spanky did develop into a respectable little bird dog just as Lester had promised.

Meanwhile Jules was going nuts! He carried on for hours, barking and howling, while I worked with Spanky. I had locked him up in an aluminum dog box and somewhere along the line he decided to dismantle it with his teeth. When I returned, I checked him for injuries and noticed that his canines were now completely silver. Obviously, gnawing on aluminum results in the metal becoming imbedded in the tooth's enamel. "Ho hum...looks like he's been to the dentist – maybe got himself some flashy new caps," I mused.

That night at supper old W.J. really got wound up. Sometime during the meal, he leaned over and with a sly wink, said to me where everyone could hear, "Son, that's some real poison ya got over there," motioning to Jules sitting beside me...(In case you didn't already know, Jules accompanied me everywhere.) "Yep, he did a mighty fine job on that big covey this afternoon. Son, that dog's got style!"

"Gee, thanks Lester, that's kind of you to say," I gushed, really beginning to enjoy the evening.

After another healthy shot of the giggle juice, Lester continued the ruse. "I've got a doctor over in Minden; promised him I'd find him a nice little Brittany just like your Jules dog."

"Oh..." I replied incredulously.

"I tell you what: I'll give you $1000 cash money for him right now." Lester said with a sly wink. Turning to Blake, W.J. confided, "I think he's a F-I-N-E little bird dog. What do you think, Bub?"

If ever anyone was in a tight spot it was Blake. On the one hand, he could tell W.J. what he really thought of Jules or any other dog I might have, for that matter. Such an outpouring

would surely cost me a cool grand, if of course I was in a selling mood (Ha!), plus risk possible humiliation for himself, since W.J. Lester was, after all, our reining bird dog guru and Blake's hero of the day. If anybody was a fair judge of dog power, surely it was Lester. Blake took the only real option left to him, "If you say so, W.J. ... and he can really cover that ground, too!"

Jules must have sensed that Blake was talking about him because he immediately went over to Blake for a nice head rub. With a groan, Blake reluctantly complied, briskly rubbing Jules' little head, thereby exposing his shiney new silver canines. "What's this, Simmons...?" Blake questioned, his eyes bulging, "your dog's teeth; are those some sort of silver inlays or what?" By now everyone at the table was examining Jules' mouth in complete amazement, and looking to me for an explanation. With little hesitation, I responded: "Blake, if you had a quality dog like Jules, wouldn't you want to take care of his dental needs? I personally recommend Doctor Robert Rockerfeller, Dentist."

Chapter 9
The Rock

The Rock, Dr. Robert Rockerfeller, always said with acrimony that he would never have gotten back into bird hunting if it had not been for Jules Verne. How true! Not because he admired "my little French ferret," hardly, but according to him, more out of desperation! "Wayne," he'd drawl, "I'm not going to walk one more step behind any shoe shining, Brittany spaniel of yours. I'm getting us some real bird dogs, ones that'll cover ground, find more birds — Pointers!" I loved it. I even started calling Jules "The King" to further infuriate him. You see, above all else, Rocky prided himself in his efficiency, particularly back in the office. He was an excellent dentist; no one can deny that, but he also loved to hear that cash drawer sliding back and forth with regularity. Rocky was a "pointer man" and nothing Jules Verne could ever do would satisfy him.

The last day of the Arkansas quail season was especially telling. As usual, the occasion began with lunch at Gene Davis' grocery store in Bradley where many of our Arkansas bird hunts originated. Gene, a veteran bird hunter of considerable note in our area, personally knew the exact location of every covey of Bobwhite quail within a fifty mile radius of his store. His only problem was that his wife, Miss Christine, kept him pretty much chained to the cash register throughout the hunting season. Getting to any of those tempting coveys seemed to be a real impossibility for him. Gene was always good for at least one new covey destination per visit provided he

was approached properly. "The Approach" was one of Rocky's specialties. It required that we drift up to the cash register together, hats in hand, the look of total and absolute dejection on both our faces. The Rock would then begin, "Gene, we hate to prevail upon you once again, *after all that's not our style*, but we are having the darnedest time finding any birds — If you would be ever so kind as to divulge just one more covey for us then we would be so grateful, (*etc.*)?" Rock's pitiful requests were usually met with that familiar dead pan look. The dread silence would ensue — (now for the excruciating wait!). If we stood there long enough, the tension would usually build enough to cause Gene to break down and slowly reach across the counter to his note pad and the long-awaited map. "Okay, Rocky, now go on up here to "bullshit corner" (a civil engineering nightmare that featured a nonsensical intersection of seven intersecting farm roads?), and take that third right before you get to the last left? Now go …. (*blah, blah, blah.*)"

A few hours later, as the sun was setting on another beautiful late winter's day, Jules found and pointed yet another one of Gene's birds for the Rock.

As usual, Rocky was trying to get a rise out of me by uttering insults as he casually walked in behind his nemesis' low slung, cat-like point. "Wayne, you've only got one bird dog here, really… you know that don't you? Spanky's your dog! Oh, and I just love the way she looks… like a fluffy little sheep out there on the horizon; just loping along at that steady pace of hers. You need to go ahead and work up a catchy sales ad for Jules next week in the *Thrifty Nickel* — and I wouldn't be looking for too much money, either!" The Rock's audacity could be positively jaw-dropping! "Now don't roll those monkey eyes at me, Jules Verne," he drawled, while brushing past the pointed dog. "You're probably lying, anyway." After the flush, and as the bird towered high above the naked plum trees, Rocky rolled him neatly. "Now that's the way to end the season!" crowed the Rock, puffing away on his stogie. "Fetch him up, Jules, and be quick about it. We don't have all day." As poor little Jules dutifully retrieved his detractor's prize, Rocky turned, and with a smirk, offhandedly remarked, "You know what; you might consider offering free shipping with Jules. Free Shipping — now that just might work!" I had to confess that this was near perfection. The "vision" of Rocky shooting yet another bird over "The King's" back would be emblazoned in *both* our minds for months to come. I would remind him of it often.

And remind him, I did, but for Jules pay-back had to wait until the following bird season when the Rock's sense of order came back to haunt him. By then Rocky had found his dream pointer. Her name was Jan and, to be sure, she was a fine little dog. We were "living the high life," the Rock with his new dog, Jan and I with Jules and Spanky. As further testament to our good fortune, we had for the first time a tremendous bird lease out near Big Spring, Texas.

The trip began inauspiciously enough with a small group of us traveling convoy style out to our new hunting destination. We were to be joined by some friends from Chicago on this particular outing, so a slight detour was required while going through Dallas. Ordinarily we'd make the eight-hour drive in one grueling episode which included a NASCAR style refueling stop in Sweetwater and a burger (if we were lucky). The Rock, our self-appointed pit boss, timed every facet of the trip — one delay anywhere along the line meant "no lunch — just a snack!" It's amazing what grown men will put up with for just a few extra minutes in the field!

Upon finding that our friends' flight had been delayed,

we decided to have a bite to eat at the airport while we waited. The day was pretty well shot by then anyway, so why not enjoy the trip? I had a couple of beers with lunch and immediately the "the prospect of a nap" overcame me. The rest of the guys were sitting as a small group, chatting it up, but talk was not something I was interested in. Instead, I found a nice quiet little spot away from everyone on the far side of our end of the terminal. I could see everyone just fine from my new vantage point. Now for a little shuteye!

Regrettably, the seating you'll find at Dallas/Fort Worth International Airport is designed more for the energetic traveler than those requiring sleep. If a simple nap is anywhere in your short term plan then you'd better consider getting a room. The problem: no headrests! My head was bobbing,

"Baby" 18x24

wobbling and rolling around like a cheap duck decoy in a windstorm! There is nothing that gets me more out of sorts than to be sleepy and have no where to rest my head. Desperation was setting in. I needed some relief! Here I was, seated at the end of a thirty-foot row of interlocking chrome chairs with a small table separating every third and fourth seat. The table, I assumed, represented a standard separation in the chain of seating. A pleasant little lady sat midway down my row of chairs enjoying a subway sandwich while her husband and children who were seated across from her, enthusiastically discussed their family's European vacation. *How exhausting!* To my right, approximately three feet off my shoulder, stood an immense fuchsia colored, carpeted wall. I stared at the wall longingly. I hate to sound priggish but ordinarily, I would find such a sight an affront to the senses, but in this case, shag carpeting never looked so good! I reasoned that if only I could rest my head against the wall's luxurious "pillowy" exterior, then sweet slumber would be assured. But in order to accomplish this, I would have to pick up my chair (and those few connected to it, I assumed?) and then move them all approximately thirty inches toward the wall. With five hundred potential witnesses surrounding me, I reasoned that a certain degree of cautious care would be a good idea since I really didn't want to create a spectacle. First I stood up and stretched a little, trying to look as nonchalant and inconspicuous as possible. Then, when I was sure no one was looking, I spun around and grabbed the chair that I had just been sitting on under my arm, as you would a rolled-up carpet, and lifted. I was stunned at the sheer weight and enormity of what I held. Had I dislodged the very geological stratum that supports Dallas, Texas? Now to move my load a mere thirty inches! I staggered forward one step, teetering! It was as if conversations around me were suddenly frozen in time? Was that my imagination? Had people stopped what they were doing and were now watching me? Was my peripheral vision confirming all this? Naturally, I ignored it all, and staggered one more impossible step. It was then I heard the woman's voice, the lady behind me imploring, "Sir, if you'll only wait till I finish my sandwich, I'll help you drag all these chairs anywhere you want to go!" Now, looking over my shoulder behind me, I could see with horror the nice lady down the way, a half-eaten subway sandwich still clutched in her little paw, her eyes perfectly round like the pepperoni slices she had been savoring. She was now seated three feet up in the air on a rigid line of airport chairs, with me of course, creating her dilemma. Like a little bird perched high on a telephone wire, she hovered there above the terminal floor. I noted her expression; still pleasant, even vaguely amused. Across from her, husband and children alike were transfixed, the children gawking at me in horror: *Where is that lunatic going with our Mother?*

While reuniting the family, I attempted to prove my sanity by using all manner of exaggerated apologies and effervescent flourishes. It was really quite a show. As we all became bosom buddies, I noticed that I was no longer sleepy at all. In fact, sleep was the furthest thing from my mind. I did begin to worry, however, that our friends' flight had arrived and that our convoy was now half way to Big Spring. So saying my grand farewells, I looked beyond my new best friends, and began searching for my own party. There they were sitting over there in the same location I'd left them, only now I noticed something quite interesting: almost to the last man, they were all in a near comatose state, enjoying the kind of sweet repose I had only imagined. Like babies they slept, all except for one: the Rock, peering directly at me over those wire-rimmed spectacles of his, that little condescending smirk on his face, slowly shaking his head. As I approached, Rocky nudged one of my comrades and I heard him say, "Here comes Simmons, back from accosting poor innocent women. Somebody really needs to call security!"

Finally, late in the afternoon the boys arrived and we got underway — just in time for supper! The Rock was getting testy. And to further complicate matters, our arrival at the ranch house that night was a little later than we had hoped, so everyone wound up sleeping-in the next morning. These were not conditions the Rock tolerated very well. His "sense of order" had been shaken and that order would have to be restored.

This was a point in our evolution when the Rock, "Mr. Efficiency," started including his yellow lab, "Star Baby", with us on our bird hunting forays. Rocky concluded that with Baby's help we could easily boost our weekend take by at least 10%. No one could deny her credentials; she was an accomplished gun dog and she certainly loved to retrieve — liked to eat, too! Earlier in the duck season, she absolutely

inhaled an eight pound Speckledbelly goose of mine while we had lunch, leaving me little more than a couple of flight feathers to puzzle over. Yep, Baby was a major player, alright. Heck, why not give her full credit: Baby wound up stealing the show!

I remember it was the first afternoon of our stay. Rocky and I and our four dogs were just cresting a cactus-covered hilltop on the north side of the lease when all hell broke loose!

To our horror a skunk scurried out from under a nearby log with Baby in close pursuit. Tripping over one another, Rocky and I and the other dogs immediately backed off, but not Baby — oh no! On about her fifth stride she caught up with that skunk and, with one big goose-gulping bite, took him square in the middle of his back. Meanwhile the Rock, recognizing a deteriorating situation, was doing his best to call off his dog.

"Leave it! Leave it, Baby!" he commanded, but to no avail. Finally, in hysterical desperation, he began spitting out all manner of commands, some of 'em laced with words no young lab needs to hear. But things were about to get even uglier when, to our dismay we realized that Baby had no interest in harming the skunk at all but instead intended to retrieve it!

Now some dogs are better retrievers than others, Baby happened to be among the best, having been meticulously trained by the Rock to carry (whatever) all the way to hand, no matter what. At that moment her master was speaking in tongues while moon-walking across the Texas landscape. Luckily Jules and I were out of harm's way. Having recognized that we were not Baby's primary focus, we intentionally zigged when Rocky zagged, thus allowing us a front row seat to the smelly scenario that was unfolding. Meanwhile Rocky was running headlong through the cactus, screaming out incoherent commands with Baby circling joyously with her new striped friend hissing and spewing for all he was worth. They ran and they ran. The skunk's blistering aroma was stifling! Around and around that hilltop Rocky went, screaming and screaming — screamed like a woman he did, until finally so exhausted, he could run no more. The best he could do was stagger and beg! "Please, Baby, please — please leave it". Baby was having the time of her life. As she danced around the Rock, she seemed to be doing some intense training of her own, "Yes, Daddy, now take it... take it to hand!" At that moment, I looked down at Jules and from his pleased expression I knew then that he enjoyed hunting with the Rock as much as I did.

Comical situations seem to follow the Rock like no one I've ever known. Once in South Arkansas, Rocky, Jules and I huddled under the onslaught of an early October Northern; watching and shooting into endless flights of doves, fresh in from who knows where. I recall Rocky was underdressed for the occasion, so he sought out our old friend, Denis Ricou, for assistance. Denis, an older gentleman who was hunting across the field from us, is one of the great Brittany enthusiasts of all time. Denis apologized to Rocky for his lack of preparation (always courtly, a Southern gentleman to the end). "No Rocky, I'm sorry I don't have any extra clothes for you. But, perhaps if we look into the back of my truck, we'll find something there to protect you from the elements." Denis then directed Rocky to his dog box where, after digging around in one of the compartments a moment, he proudly presented

him with a filthy, excrement-incrusted electric blanket that had been there as long as he had owned the vehicle. The Rock, never one to be finicky, quickly cut a hole in the center of the pink blanket and slipped it over his head. An old leather belt was then cinched-up tight around his waist. And, voila! The ensemble was complete. Truly, this was one of the most bizarre sights ever witnessed in the annals of the sport. Thank Goodness, they didn't have an electrical outlet handy. Broken wires protruded everywhere! Then, true to form, Denis reached into his old, tattered hunting coat and produced the ever-present pint of Courvoisier that resided there.

Denis, with his happy little round face and jaunty tweed shooting hat, was to me the very picture of what an old French poacher was supposed to look like. And why not: that's what he was! Then came the magical question, "Care to kiss the baby, Rocky?" The old gentleman had covered this ground before. Rocky was very cold, but hypothermia had little to do with their bonding ritual. The Rock's eyes rolled back in his head as he lifted the cold bottle to his lips. Ah, yes, the boys "kissed the baby" repeatedly that morning.

Mental images of the Rock, braced against the cold north wind, puffing on his cigar, still delight me to this day. Firing like a mad man, he wore his soiled, hot pink, flannel serape victoriously — with its dozens of naked, broken black wires sticking out at odd angles, he was to the world and to the doves some strange Medusa from hell.

Chapter 10

Escapades with the Little Frenchman

There was a time when all our outdoor sporting events included Denis Ricou, the little Frenchman. Trout fishing on the White, turkey hunting, squirrel hunting, surf fishing on the coast, you name it, and we did it. Especially bird hunting! We were like the Three Musketeers — four Musketeers, if you include my old childhood friend, Paul Thornton who lived in Dallas. At that time, we were pretty much an all-Brittany crew. Of course, back then in the beginning, at least, the Rock didn't have any pointers. He just tagged along, complaining bitterly every step of the way. But that was OK. It was just part of the fun.

Remember, dear reader, when I confessed earlier that, under the right circumstances, Jules Verne could be lead a hair or two astray? Well, the right circumstances usually involved Denis' two Brittany bitches, Speck and Su Su, sometimes known as "the Darlings," or more appropriately, "the Pole Cat Sisters" (no relation to Baby, but definitely they were cut from the same cloth). These two walked the seamy side, all right. If either one of them had ever experienced formal training it was long forgotten. Their Master prescribed to a more spontaneous approach (Anything goes!). According to Denis it was perfectly acceptable for a Brittany spaniel to divert at any time from our game of choice (bobwhite quail) to pursue other prey. His reasoning was simple; their breeding demanded it.

You see, the Brittany spaniel as a hunting breed was developed in France several hundred years ago among the peasants of Brittany. They were bred to do it all: point and retrieve, even track. They were playful and friendly, great with kids, as suitable around the home as they were in the field. Since the game-rich lands of that day were in large measure controlled by the aristocracy, poaching was a way of life. These naughty Frenchmen required a "poacher's dog": compact in size and ultra obedient. Since they never knew when they and their close working hunting companion would be forced to slide quietly back over a fence or through a bordering hedgerow, these dogs were bred to point surely and retrieve quickly. Above all else, the Brittany was bred to be a superior hunter — and to be versatile. They reasoned, I guess, that a bunny in the pot was just about as good as a partridge on the grill. Enter Denis Ricou, rightful heir to his ancestor's handiwork: the Brittany spaniel, and to my way of thinking, the last man on this earth willing to curb a Brittany's natural instincts.

So, ironically, Denis was actually a purist. He had traveled extensively, hunting and fishing all over the British Isles and on the Continent. I understand he spent quite a lot of time in the very district in France where his family originated, learning the art of "rough shooting*" as it is called in Europe. And he had the shooting skills and the dog power to do it up right, back here in the States. Nothing would make Denis happier than to go out with "his darlings" and bag three or four quail, a woodcock, half dozen snipe and a few hares. Throw in an alligator and a sack full of robins and he'd really have something to write home about!

Above all else, Denis believed in paying his own way. He nonchalantly confided once that he always carried a pocket full of five-dollar bills with him whenever he went hunting, just in case one of his girls put him in a compromising position. We'll never know how many farmers came home to find one of his prized hens splayed out on the front porch, stone cold dead, anchoring a crisp five-dollar bill. A jaunty little Frenchman in a tweed chapeau, no doubt, would be seen skulking off into the brush with his demoiselles in tow. Forget the Farm Bureau; Denis Ricou was himself a one-man farm subsidy program!

The Hill Country of Central Texas is a beautiful area for the outdoorsman, and in wet years it literally teems with wildlife. Mother Nature has smiled on this land. Over the years the "Four Musketeers" spent many, many enjoyable days here, soaking in her bountiful gifts. Bobwhite quail were our main quarry; we'd hunt them throughout the day in the rocky, mesquite-strewn hills and draws. The birds as well as the deer and turkey were normally in abundance. Ducks were a bonus. We'd jump and shoot them off the many creeks and tanks found in that region. In the evenings we'd sit around a roaring campfire and drink brandy and tell tall tales, and relive the extraordinary things we had witnessed that day. I remember Jules would sit there beside me for hours. His head was always situated directly under my hand. Every so often he would throw his muzzle up, prodding me to rub his head or scratch his ear.

Where the taking of any type of game animal is permissible

These were good times. I recall it was on one of these outings that we witnessed some particularly amazing Brittany work. Denis' ancestors, no doubt, would have been especially proud as his "femmes fatales" had headlined the event.

As I recall, we had five Brittanys down; too many, in my opinion to hunt effectively, but just enough if you're looking for trouble. Denis' darlings started the action by picking up the trail of a big jackrabbit buck. They flushed it on the far side of the line and pushed it all the way across in front of us, picking up Thornton's dog, Bud, along the way, then Spanky and finally Jules. By the time "the pack" had reached the top of the hill they were in full cry. They would have put a pack of beagles to shame. Denis was ecstatic. "Get him, girls!" he hollered, "Now whatever you do, don't let him get away!" I was in shock! Was that Jules — baying? In no time, their barking became fainter until finally they were no longer in hearing. We looked at one another

"Hillside Flush" 12x24

in amazement. It was getting late. So late, in fact, that Thornton and I were becoming a little concerned. The Texas Hill Country is no place to be at night, especially if you're a dog. Denis wasn't the least bit worried though. His girls could handle anything out there. Denis was probably taking mental measurements of his den floor in preparation for the new bear skin rug his girls were no doubt working on. Meanwhile, the rest of us were discussing our options when the Rock cocked his head and motioned for quiet; then he grimaced and dryly reported, "Bad News — I think they're coming back!" Then we all heard 'em, their beautiful music getting louder and louder until finally our beloved hounds seemed to be just over the next hill. All our eyes were now glued on the crest. We fully expected to see one tired rabbit come bouncing over the top but to our amazement, it wasn't a bunny at all, but a herd of deer that boiled over the hill with our Brittanys in quick pursuit. Denis now was in absolute ecstasy... rigors of delight coursed through his body. He pounded Rocky's back as he reached into his coat for the ever-present bottle of Courvoisier; "I am so proud of my darlings. They'll get double rations tonight, for sure! Please make a note of that, Rocky?" (For some reason, Rocky and I were always expected to feed Denis' dogs whenever we were on an outing. To this day I have no clue as to why — maybe it was a seniority thing? In any event, we didn't mind. It was just a strange ritual that became part of the drill.)

Perhaps, patient reader, you've recognized striking similarities between Denis' dogs and my own. I admit, there were troubling parallels, but genetics will do that. Our dogs were far from perfect, but they loved to hunt and were sweet companions. And because of them, life for both Denis and me has been far richer.

The little Frenchman has always been one of my favorites. I can still picture him sitting there at our campfire, surrounded by his adoring Brittanys and cradling a beautiful Ansley Fox double with its elegant gold embossed receiver. The gun, a sixteen gauge, featured a flying quail on one side and a hovering woodcock on the other. Denis is to this day an excellent shot, a trusted companion, a superb chef, a veritable fountain of sporting knowledge and the man most responsible for my early interest in the Brittany spaniel breed.

"Greta and Soula" 30x36

Chapter 11
The Reunion

In my house, when it came time to go hunting, a quiet departure was always preferable to one where there was a lot of fanfare. That was just asking for trouble. "Not again; didn't you just get back? Have the leaves been raked? How about those Christmas lights — the garage, it's a disgrace," etc.! Some of my friends could get by with more amicable, civilized farewells from their spouse where they were presented with a freshly baked pie or something, but not me. Nah, just a quiet "now he's here, now he's not", worked out the best. I liked to think of myself as smoke slipping out through a cracked door.

It was early December and well before Christmas. On the afternoon in question, my exit was a little sloppier than usual. No doubt, rusty from lack of use — I hadn't been hunting in days. Gay was well aware of my plans, though. We'd whipped the hair and hide off that dog for hours the evening before. I was no match for her arguing skills. She was the reigning queen of debate, having never ever given an inch during any one of our contests. Perhaps if my positions had been more sustainable then my win ratio would have improved, you may wonder? Who knows? At any rate, at times like these, she'd generally close the show by interjecting something poignant. In this case it was a thoughtful, salient question, delivered point blank and broadside. "Years from now," she whispered with quiet resignation in her voice, "when you're on your death bed, or maybe lying out in some desolate, frozen field or marsh somewhere, breathing your last, will your final thoughts be of your bird dogs or the ducks? Or will your last thoughts be of the girls and me? I'd really like to know." As always, I was rendered speechless; a little saddened, too — but as always,

still committed to the hunt.

Later, just as Jules and I were about to successfully evaporate into the great out of doors, Hattie Grant, an occasional member of our household, glanced up from her work as we were making our escape. Too late!

Hattie Taylor Grant was in her early eighties at the time. She had been with Gay's family, the Jacobs, since near childhood, and was as much a part of the Jacobs clan as anyone, especially the "brought-ins" (i.e., "the in-laws"). Hattie was the granddaughter of a slave. She was, hands down, the hardest working human being that ever drew breath and she had a critical, all-seeing eye. Hattie helped raise our children, as she had Gay and her siblings before them, and Gay's mother and her sisters before them. She was integral: as critical to life as we knew it in our small provincial southern hometown, as say — Mammaw, the Family Matriarch (I still shudder). Hattie used to say that Gay's grandfather had "great balls of sense between his ears he ain't even used yet." I think she had her share, too. Once she casually remarked that there was something in the human condition that caused men to naturally hate anyone they had unfairly wronged. At the time, that seemed to me a startling, prophetic realization: a truism — one, frankly, that I'd never really considered. Hattie was insightful that way.

As was normally the case, Hattie was standing there in the kitchen at the ironing board, engrossed in one of her enthusiastic, heart to heart conversations with none other than herself. She looked up from her meticulous ironing and saw Jules and me standing there; me fumbling with the doorknob and making lame sounding excuses as to where I was off to, and Jules simply tugging away like a madman. Hattie, ever so slowly, shook her head and went on about her endless work, still mumbling almost inaudibly to herself. "Laudie, there goes that Mr. Medlock again... Umm, umm, umm, when he leaves this world, life ain't gonna owe him nothin'!" For some reason,

Hattie always confused my name with that of my wife's aunt's second husband, Medlock Harbison. The two of us were somehow interchangeable.

Late in life, Medlock joined the Jacobs' coterie as Tutor's second husband. "Mr. Medlock" was thirty years my senior, a quick southern gentleman who puffed on a pipe constantly. His sense of humor was kind of quirky and dry — very dry (except when wetted down with his favorite brand of whiskey, Southern Comfort). Medlock was a "brought-in" from Arkansas, as I was a "brought-in" from Tennessee. By the way, my wife coined this quaint, differentiating moniker in an effort, I suspect, to elicit in me insecure feelings of non-permanency. Medlock and I were outsiders and our continuance was negotiable. Hattie's was not, however. No matter what happened, Hattie stayed.

In any event, I kind of liked Hattie's take on my approach to life. Mental images of me "drinking that last delicious drop from Life's Golden Goblet" had a certain cavalier air I found appealing. Normally, I would have stuck around for more insightful hints, but knowing that the "War Department" was lurking somewhere close by didn't allow me time to dawdle. A nuclear exchange with Gay directly preceding one of the big hunts of the year was no way to kick things off.

We arrived at the lease late that night. Jim and George Fritze rode with me; Fred Berry and Mr. Medlock rode with Rocky. We were enjoying a strong pot of coffee the next morning, just relaxing, sipping our coffee and making plans for the morning when lo and behold, David Rhoden, our lease partner from Waco appeared unexpectedly with his eighteen-year-old son, David Junior.

Now here was a striking pair. Both, handsome like Greek gods, they worked out at least four hours a day in order to maintain their incredible Adonis physiques. David, slightly shorter than his son who stood a towering six feet, four inches, would proudly tell us that back at the gym, he was known

simply as "David" and his son... "Mr. Rhoden". Expensive sunglasses always graced their finely chiseled faces in the field, and brightly colored headbands held back their luxurious dark curls. Walking across a shimmering sage field behind those graceful setters of theirs, they always looked to me more like movie stars than bird hunters.

Oh, and Big David was constantly up to something. He and the Rock had been roommates in dental school and, according to Rocky, even at that early, impressionable age David was forever playing devious tricks on his innocent classmate; a master of deceit then as he is today. Rocky attempted to provide his friend with moral guidance but to no avail. Today, David's professional specialty is so predictable: tooth implantation — how could it be anything else! Oh, and he had made millions at it, too! Although once again, according to the Rock, our loyal reporter, "most of his patients ultimately return, paper bag in hand, teeth in bag." Oh, how it saddened the Rock. This to some may sound like professional jealousy at work: two highly competitive, A-Plus personalities vying for the same toothsome dollars, but I am assured by the Rock, our "Moral Compass," that nothing could be farther from the truth.

"You know what," David began, "it just occurred to me that we have an even number of hunters here this weekend, with all the members present, too. Wouldn't it be fun to divide up and have some sort of friendly contest, maybe where the team who bags the most birds this morning is treated to supper by the losers? Hey, what do you think about that?" I must have still been in a fog from the long drive the night before because I, too, enthusiastically agreed to the wager.

That's all David needed. With customary audacity, he quickly picked *his* "A Team" which included himself, David, Jr., Rocky and Fred (all basic predators). The leftovers (men of integrity), our "B Team," included Medlock, the Fritze boys and myself.

As the "A Team" pulled away in their vehicles there was the usual bantering. They were confident of success, and why not? All four of 'em were pretty fair shots, plus, they had Fred, or more importantly Fred's dogs. Fred was a professional bird dog trainer and his dog power was legendary. We were going to have to rely on Jules, Spanky and a couple of broke and semi-broke pointers. Maybe Jules would work some magic. "The Fritze Boys" were certainly capable of it — this father-son team could really shoot. Why, all Medlock and I had to do was run along behind them, scooping up the bobwhites as they fell from the sky! Or so I thought.

Our dogs did their share that morning and so did the Fritze boys. Medlock and I fell a little short, though. After an hour or so, it became apparent that we were going to have to either tighten up on our shooting or get ready to pay for dinner. By my count neither Medlock, nor I had bagged a single bird (out of maybe a box of shells?) This was poor shooting by any standard and I apologized to them all for my lousy performance. I then looked at Medlock, halfway expecting him to acknowledge his complicity in the matter. As usual, Medlock's measured response was "Classic Medlock". Puffing away on his pipe, he casually responded, "Oh, having a bad day, are you? I personally am doing some of my best shooting." Subject closed.

Medlock Harbison was born in Helena, Arkansas in the year 1920. Before World War II he attended the University of Arkansas at Fayetteville where he studied geology. Naturally, after graduation, Medlock went into the oil business and while still in his twenties, ran for and won a seat in the Arkansas State Senate. Medlock spent only one term as an Arkansas State Senator. According to him, it wasn't to his liking.

"Never underestimate the stupidity of the American public!" he once ranted after watching David Duke, ex-KKK Grand Wizard and official state embarrassment, make the Louisiana Governor's race run-off. Further proof of his thesis, he maintained, came almost forty years after he left politics. While traveling through an out of the way corner of his old district, he stopped in at a dilapidated country store to buy a soft drink. Apparently, Medlock had stumped there some four generations earlier, because the old proprietor, upon recognizing the young "Senator Harbison," commented to him that he was no better than all the rest! "You never see hide or hair of 'em till election time", he raged. "So, what are you gonna do fer me this time, Senator?" Medlock swears that this happened and that he countered, "Sir, I no longer represent you in the Arkansas State Senate and, if you had any sense at all, you'd know that! I am your President, however, and I would appreciate it if you would hurry with that Big Orange!" Getting rattled, losing one's faculties: these were not in Medlock's repertoire.

Old Uncle Meddy, he could really handle it. Once, during the summer of '80 he proved to me just how totally unflappable he really was. Our families were vacationing together in Wisconsin at my wife's family's "summer retreat" in Ephraim. While there Medlock and I had occasion to go fishing together. It was a hot sultry day, the Fourth of July as I recall, and it turned into a very memorable afternoon for many reasons. Not because we had a great day of fishing exactly, although we did, but because of what happened at the dock in Gills Rock afterwards.

The plan was that Gay and her Aunt Tutor would meet us at the boat dock that afternoon. When they arrived Medlock was in a state of euphoria. He had caught a trophy rainbow trout and he intended to have it mounted. The girls were happily taking pictures of his catch when out of nowhere appeared this drunken woman who, using the foulest language imaginable, proceeded to berate my wife unmercifully for accidentally blocking in her car with ours.

Gay was very apologetic and terrified! I myself was speechless, having never witnessed such an outburst from any woman... or man, for that matter; not even on one of our sporting events. It was the unflappable Medlock who came to the rescue, though.

Stepping forward, his pipe clenched tightly between his teeth, Medlock said in his most haughty manner (which could be pretty condescending), "Excuse me madam, but just what rock did you crawl out from under?" That halted the diatribe mid-"Mother blankety, blank". Obviously stung by Medlock's remark, the woman spun around and stormed off, at which time Medlock simply shrugged, turned to Gay and with total disdain said, "Ha! Obviously not a Vassar girl!" Never breaking stride, Medlock now with pipe smoke totally obscuring the dock, proceeded to tell us that if the woman had had any class at all, she would have at least congratulated him on his trophy before she left. Then Medlock abruptly stopped admiring his own fish and began eyeing covetously the fish I was holding. "Wait just a minute," he whispered, "I think your fish is bigger than mine." Medlock then reached out grabbed my trout which was slightly larger and handed me his own. And to this day, "my" once-in-a-lifetime trophy trout, caught fair and square, resides on a wall at the Jacobs' cottage with a little brass plaque underneath, emblazoned with Medlock's triumphant words:

"13 1/2 lb. Rainbow Trout - Caught off Door County, Wisconsin
In the year of the Hegira 1358, by Medlock Harbison,
World's Foremost Fisherman - Olympic Gin Rummy Player
Bon Vivant, and truly - One of Nature's Noblemen"

Meanwhile back at the ranch...
We arrived at the designated hour to find "A" Team smugly sitting around the kitchen table, waiting. "Well, how did "B" team do?" questioned a confident David Rhoden.

"I believe well enough to bury you guys!" George crowed.

"Thirty-one by actual count, and they're in the ice chest outside if anyone cares to check," Medlock countered, his pipe working overtime.

"Oh no, we trust you." David cooed, "After all, if you can't trust your friends, then just who can you trust? Right? Let's count 'em up, boys."

One after the other, the "A" Team members emptied their game bags on the table, all except for Fred, who was still outside seeing to his dogs.

"20, 21, 22 and 23... That's all!" tallied the Rock. At that exact moment, Fred burst through the door carrying an exceptionally heavy-looking game bag.

"Well, how did the *armateurs* do?" Fred Berry inquired, with his usual folksy charm.

"We did alright, but more importantly, how did you do?" Jim Fritze asked.

"Well, I can show you better'n I can tell you. One, two, three, four, five, six, seven, eight, nine...and ten. Good enough?"

Yes, indeed! Good enough. A dejected "B" Team glumly sat there. We had actually lost by three birds.

"But Fred, normally you're more interested in working your dogs than you are in shooting quail," I questioned.

"Old Fred does what he's called upon to do." he solemnly answered.

After lunch and a nap, an increasingly annoying David Rhoden kept reminding us gratuitously about "our dinner plans". "Oh, and by the way, we took care of our birds from this morning." He said, "You guys ought to clean yours, too. You'll be too tired after supper and you won't feel up to it then."

"Thanks for the advice, but we don't have time for that now. We're here to hunt!"

We were prepared to buy dinner, as any good sportsmen

"Bailey's Harbor Browns" 16x20

"Portrait of a Thoroughbred" 8x10

would, but we weren't about to let David Rhoden dictate any more of our activities. Enough was enough!

That evening during dinner I sat next to Medlock and Fred. They were always entertaining, particularly after a few drinks. As a fresh bottle of Merlot drifted by our end of the table, Medlock picked up the bottle, examined the label and poured himself a glass. Ordinarily this was far from unusual behavior for Medlock, who could really put it away. But for someone who had just the previous week given up the stuff under some duress, I might add, it was a little discomforting to watch.

As Medlock slowly lifted the glass to his lips, he stopped just short of touch down and turned to me, saying, "Perhaps Gay told you that I gave up drinking last week."

"As a matter of fact, Medlock, she did mention something along those lines," I cautiously said.

"Well, I didn't like it." Medlock replied dryly.

Upon hearing that, Fred, as familiar as anyone with that age-old quandary, countered that his wife also had recently complained that he was going to have to "get some help with his drinking".

To which I said, as if on cue, "And what did you say to that, Fred?"

"Why, I told her I didn't need any help with my drinking. I could handle that little chore pretty well on my own," Fred chuckled. The evening continued at this pace for quite a while.

Toast after self-gratifying toast was suffered through by "B" team. Most of these insufferable diatribes were directed at "A" Team's superlative accomplishments of the day. It was enough to make you want to give up bird hunting — or at least drinking! As far as I was concerned, "A" Team's crowning achievement was their ability to order every visible item on the menu and then drink the joint dry.

We knew the end was near with the Rock's final toast.

"Friends, I'd like to honor one of our recently fallen comrades, John Mason who died last year. He was..."

"Oh, no!" Fred groaned, genuinely grief stricken. "You mean he's dead? Why didn't somebody tell me?"

The Rock shook his head, and with his usual unique brand of sarcasm replied, "I'm sorry, Fred I thought you knew of his passing — you being a pallbearer at his funeral and all."

Later, back at the ranch, as the "A" Team prepared for bed, "B" team grudgingly prepared to dress a huge pile of birds. Not cleaning them after lunch had indeed been a big mistake. We knew it. And someone else knew it, too. "Now if you had only listened to me, you wouldn't have to spend the rest of the night doing this," David gloated, his speech slightly garbled due to the toothbrush protruding from his mouth. With a quick swipe of a towel he exposed those beautiful, pearly whites (probably all capped), and bid us good night. "And thank you again for a wonderful evening. Good night to you all, and please keep the noise down."

"Tight... Tight...Tight..." That was Fred's mantra, the words hauntingly familiar, referring to his condition and chanted repeatedly after a few too many cocktails. "Tight...Tight... Tight... But Ole Fred's not about to abandon you boys — even though somehow, I've taken drunk!"

No, he would stay up with us until the job was done, offering moral support and spirited conversation, he and his steady companion, Jack in the Black. Was I hallucinating, or was that pile over there getting bigger?

We had an assembly line working: picking, gutting, washing and then packaging quail for the freezer. Fred did most of the talking. He lectured us on the shaky future of bird hunting and the best ways to reintroduce quail to areas where habitat was lost then restored, using pen raised birds and specially-built protective brush piles. Nah, he didn't believe that it would work worth a nickel, but just the same, it'd occupy your time in the off-season. I always found Fred to be immensely entertaining and the subjects he covered vastly interesting. But then I'm a bird hunter. I especially liked his points of wisdom on which bird dog traders you could trust (essentially only himself), and those you should avoid (all others).

All the while, Jules Verne sat there next to Fred, waiting for and accepting those occasional head rubs and bouncing his hand violently in his own inimitable way with his nose when the hand went still.

"Son, when are you gonna run old Jules here in another field trial?" Fred asked, feigning serious interest. Whatever my expression, it sent him off into rigors of howling laughter. Regaining his composure for a second, Fred then asked me to recount for him one more time the story of how "Little Jules *almost* walked away with the gold."

"Alright," I said, knowing full well that Fred knew the story as well as I did. He just loved to hear it retold, especially when there were those around who hadn't yet heard it.

"Well, one time, long years ago, when "Jules" here was just a mere pup, I entered him in a little field trial back in Shreveport," I began. "Call it misguided curiosity or maybe delusions of grandeur, but back then I really thought Jules could do pretty much whatever he wanted to do. Well, when it came time for Jules to show us what he was made of, something sort of anti-climatic happened."

"And what was that?" Fred questioned, while nodding his head slowly — eyes half closed — all knowing, a Fred Berry trademark.

"Well, he didn't score a single find. He hunted hard all through his round, but it was as if the ground in front of him had been somehow cleared of any birds for him to point — that is until we got up near the finish line."

"Oh, and now the rest of the story...." Fred added, smiling,

still nodding, eyes half closed.

"So at the finish line I lost sight of Jules momentarily. He sort of darted in behind the gallery at the last moment. Well, I just waded in after him; on through the onlookers and past the hot dog concession, where I heard some snickering. And then, there was my Little Jules, locked up solid on, of all things, a parked ATV. What in the world was he doing? I thought. Although to me it was the prettiest point I'd seen all day, I have to admit, it was still a little embarrassing. After all, bird dogs aren't supposed to point inanimate objects — especially, not at a field trial. As I walked up alongside my dog, the smell of hot dogs and hamburgers permeated the air. Surely he wasn't pointing that! I could hear the faint cackling in the crowd, the snide, insensitive remarks. Shaking my head in disbelief, I noticed that the four-wheeler had an old olive green tarp covering its unknown cargo. Jules wouldn't budge. As I lifted the edge of the canvas I could hear little chirping sounds, the sounds you occasionally hear in the field just prior to an explosive covey flush. Holy Mackerel! Jules had found the mother lode: dozens of the biggest, fattest quail you ever saw, all sitting in their little pens, awaiting their debut before the crowd. 'Point... Point,' someone yelled, laughing. Out of nowhere appeared one of the judges who, after surveying the scene and hearing from me what had happened, ruled Jules 'out of bounds'; and nothing I could say or do would change his mind."

"One more bird to go," Jim announced from the kitchen sink, holding up the last quail.

Hearing this, Fred jumped to his feet, hollering, "I can't do it! And I don't care what they say or do to me, either. You boys have been so good to me..." he whined.

We all stared at Fred in disbelief. "What in the hell are you talking about, Fred?" someone asked.

"They made me do it...Here, here let me clean that last bird for you fellers. This just ain't right!" Fred's feeble attempts to do the right thing were, of course, meant to be just that.

Even an Irish setter can smell a rat. And the biggest one of all was standing right there in front of us.

"O.K., Fred; spill it," Jim ordered.

"You won't let 'em hurt me, will you? I'm near *seventy-year-old* and you know the kinda muscles those Rhoden boys have," whined "poor old Fred".

"Yes, Fred, let's have it," Medlock fired back at him.

Fred sat back heavily in his chair. "Okay, okay, I gotta get it off my chest. My conscience is hurting me too much." Although Fred feigned distress pretty well, there still was that mischievous glint in his eye. He couldn't hide that. So in his own unique, pitiful way Fred began to unfold the entire treacherous conspiracy: "After lunch, while you boys were having your nap, Rhoden... it was Rhoden, he made me slip in here, while no one was looking, and pour all our birds from this morning into your ice chest over there," pointing to the blue Igloo in the corner. The one that only an hour or so before *seemed bottomless!* "You just cleaned all of "A" Team's birds as well as your own!" Fred said, staring at us intently. Apparently he liked what he saw, because it caused him to double over in howling laughter.

Talk about blind-sided; our team had been had, royally! "You mean we got tricked into cleaning "A" Team's kill from this morning?" George asked his father, staring at him in disbelief. "I can't believe they'd do that!" The Fritze boys were genuinely shocked and appalled by our competitor's behavior. Both George and Jim had been Eagle Scouts as boys. And although they hadn't come up with the Golden Rule on their own, they prescribed pretty much fully to it.

Actually I thought the joke was a pretty good one. I was just a little disappointed that I hadn't come up with it myself. I didn't tell them that, though. Instead, a fragile, hurt response seemed more appropriate. "I feel violated. That's how I feel."

On hearing my indignation, Fred, having regained his composure, placed his hand on my shoulder. "Son, I feel your pain. Now you just tell these boys here, Old Fred's not to be blamed."

"To think, that David Rhoden would stoop this low in order to have his birds cleaned. And to compound matters further, force this old man into his web of deceit. Well, it's despicable!" Medlock wailed. Fred was having the time of his life; sitting there, smiling — his eyes half closed, nodding in agreement. "But son, that's not the half of it..." he whispered.

"Oh!"

"At noon, when you boys were in here counting up, I was outside, remember."

"Yeah, I believe you were feeding your dogs — we know." George said.

"Feeding my dogs — yes — but that's not all I was doing out there. Rhoden had me on a mission."

All of a sudden I felt the bile rushing toward my throat. And from their sick expressions, it was obvious my teammates were experiencing unpleasant symptoms all their own.

"Son of a bitch!" Medlock murmured...

"You left your birds on the tailgate of the truck. So it really wasn't my fault. You do understand?" Fred said, looking slowly around at each and every one of us, loving every minute of it. "I just kinda helped myself to a few of them." More belly laughs from Fred. "Truth be known, you boys won a free supper fair and square. *That Rhoden's a snake!*"

We'd been set up, all right. Not once but twice! Were we that naïve or were we dealing with criminal genius here? I really thought there was gonna be a lynching.

The only thing that saved Rhoden that night was a locked door. After pounding on it and shouting insults, we dragged back into the kitchen. The Fritze boys continued the assault for a while longer, having totally lost it. In desperation they dug up an extremely noisy vacuum cleaner from somewhere and ran up and down the hall with it, making a terrible racket.

Afterwards we sat there in the kitchen plotting retribution. All our pathetic little plans for "pay-back" seemed so childishly pitiful and inept in comparison to "A" Team's brand of trickery. We were outdone and undone all at the same time.

Suddenly Rhoden's door cracked open. He stood there in the dark for a moment, behind the door, as if trying to gauge our intentions. Finally leaving the safety of his room, he ventured slowly into the kitchen while tightening his robe and lamenting his tortured sleep, "I just had a terrible nightmare. I dreamed there were those who wanted to harm me. Men were screaming my name. I was vilified. It was very disturbing. I think I'll go back to bed now." Chuckling quietly to himself, David Rhoden sauntered off to his bed, leaving "B" team to their abject misery.

"West Texas Camp House" 16x20

Chapter 12
Life and Death on the Texas Plains

Included here are four Incidents that still give me the willies anytime I start reliving them. I know in the scheme of things the events described in these little sketches may seem pretty mild to someone who has undergone serious adversity but for me these experiences (and their happy conclusions) were all I wanted.

Me and My Phobia

"Where is that little ferret?" The Rock's impatience was growing. "I saw him pussy footin' around not three minutes ago — right here, right here on the edge of this ravine, probably looking for a rat! We scanned up and down the edge of the fifty foot cliff but Jules was nowhere to be seen. And what a ravine it was: a nasty fifty-foot deep gash that sliced the rolling countryside in half. Not unusual either; the L.B.J. Grasslands Game Management Area was laced with these steep slashes, making hunting there almost intolerable.

As I craned my neck in an attempt to see over the edge, I felt that familiar unpleasant "wim-wam" sensation just north of the belt buckle, right there in the pit of my stomach. Fear of heights. It's something I've dealt with for years. My phobia on a scale of 1-10, would probably rate only a 3+ by National Mental Health Department standards, a mere blip on the screen of everyday inconveniences we work through. Usually I just glaze over the unpleasant sensation, telling myself it's simply a state of mind, a keen imagination at work. So

when it happened this time, I wasn't surprised, just a wee bit uncomfortable.

I baby-stepped in a little closer to the edge... (Ugh!) And then to my right and ten feet below the lip, I glimpsed a little patch of orange color that contrasted with the deep magenta worn by the autumn Sumac dotted underbrush. "Yep, there he is, and he's got a point, too, right there in that little clump of Sumac," I excitedly whispered to Rocky, pointing out the dog.

Jules was locked up on a little grassy ledge. Frozen rock solid, he was waiting for us to get into position. But I didn't like it. The whole setup smelled of disaster. We had four dogs out, two of them wild and inexperienced; far too many dogs to control. And how was Jules going to react when we flushed the birds? Well, one thing was certain: I'd never be able to call him off that point. Hoping to avoid further complications we moved in with dispatch. But scramble as we did, we weren't quite fast enough. Before we could get into position, Jan appeared out of nowhere and immediately backed Jules' point alongside Rocky on the canyon rim. All the while I was carefully creeping along the ledge toward Jules, hoping to get a hand on his collar and not fall off the canyon wall myself. Overhead I could hear the Rock cautioning dogs, multiple dogs now. Real concern could be heard in his voice, "Ennh, ennh! Baby, no, get in here"! As my hand closed on Jules' collar, I felt some relief but not for long. The big covey erupted all around us with a roar. I imagined I could feel those soft wingtips brushing past, gently pushing me out into the chasm. In the ensuing commotion, which included a lot of shooting from above, I saw with horror a large dark shape sailing out over my head into the void. It was Baby.

That was our last trip to LBJ. We decided then and there that we were no matches for the rough, inhospitable terrain that marked the area. The steep canyons held birds all right, but they gave 'em up far too reluctantly. We left winners, though; Baby survived her near collision with death by landing in the swollen, muddy stream below, and the Rock — well, he made a nice double as the covey passed overhead. All and all it turned into a pretty fair outing.

The Sand Burr

Hunting anywhere with a gun implies risk. We all recognize that. But, like the canyon country of L.B.J., there are other subtle pitfalls in the field that can be just as deadly as the careless handling of firearms. Would you believe that something as insignificant as a tiny sand burr could be one of them?

Once, long ago on a beautiful afternoon in West Texas, I encountered a situation that very nearly ended it for me. I was hunting all by myself that day as we often did. Early on I noticed that Jules had picked up a sand burr and was limping along, trying to get to the next birdy looking spot. As was always the case he was reluctant to stop hunting long enough for me to extract the offending burr but, after some coaxing, he finally relented and came in. Surely you remember how difficult it was to leave the swimming hole when you were a kid and your mom was hollering that supper was on the table. That's how Jules was. Anyway I pulled the burr free from his paw and during the course of the operation promptly stuck it into my own finger. If you've ever encountered a sand burr, you know how incredibly sharp the tiny thorns are that surround and protect the burr's core. These little spears are barbed, much like a porcupine's quill, and are tough to extract once you're impaled. At the time it made perfect sense to use my front teeth as a makeshift pair of tweezers (so as to not re-stick myself). So using my teeth, I extracted it a second time. Now with the sand burr firmly clasped between my teeth, I

was preparing to remove it with my free hand when without thinking; I sucked in a breath of air. At that very moment the burr slipped from its hold and was literally blown down the wind tunnel of my throat where it lodged inextricably, with a jolt! Immediately I knew I was in serious trouble: all-alone, miles from anywhere and choking to death! That tiny, insignificant little sticker: it might as well have been a cross-tie lodged in my wind pipe. Unable to breathe, gagging, and coughing, I stumbled around for a while, then decided if I was going to try something; it was going to have to be pretty quick. So, using my fingers, I started reaching and ultimately, stabbing as deeply as I could down my throat. I remember noticing the blood and thinking, "Good, maybe that'll help float the damn thing loose!" And so apparently it did, cause out it came... allowing me to once again breathe and hunt another day.

The Blizzard

Lady luck always seemed to smile on us. A West Texas blizzard once hit Thornton and me out near Breckenridge and although that in itself isn't the luckiest of scenarios, I guess the fact that we survived it with all our toes and fingers intact, is!

At the time we were day hunting an unfamiliar bird lease and, to further complicate matters, after a few hours we got hopelessly turned around. Of course we refused to concede that we were lost (and more than likely off our lease). Oh no, the birds were there, and more importantly, we were there! But eventually, even two great rationalizers like Thorny and me had to face facts: we were hopelessly lost and no doubt poaching! Since hunting without permission in Texas is the ultimate bad idea, we decided to call it a day. So under an impending blizzard, we started walking with newfound purpose. No longer were we shooting into those big beautiful coveys. Nope; we simply walked right through 'em. Our dogs

"Looks Like Dinner to Me"
12x20

seemed particularly amazed at our newfound nonchalance. But after an hour or so of cold rain, then sleet, and finally snow, even their enthusiasm for the birds was dampened. Man or beast, we all have our limits.

It must have been 9:00 or 10:00 at night and we still had no idea where we were. We were becoming dangerously hypothermic from the wet and cold. The wind kept blowing. The snow kept falling. If there were lights in the distance we couldn't see them. Jules had just finished up his first heartworm treatment a couple of months earlier, so he wasn't in the greatest of shape. He had absolutely no lanolin in his coat so he was soaked through and shivering. I recall Jules kept trying to crawl up under bushes in pitiful attempts to bed up. Finally in desperation, I wrapped him in my hunting coat and carried him for what seemed like miles until suddenly out of nowhere appeared a power line, glistening and sagging with ice in the faint evening light. That line obviously ran from somewhere to something. Problem was: it was still a 50/50 proposition as to which direction was our way out? After a little discussion and a few heated words, Thornton made a pretty good observation, "O.K. Fool, sometimes you just have to assume something. I say this way!" And that's the direction we took.

After walking only a few hundred yards we came upon what had always been a particularly ugly sight to us: an oil field pumping unit. Given the circumstances, that rusted relic from the fifties' oil boom looked pretty good to us: sort of cheery sitting there, the old iron horse head slowly moving up and then down, sucking in that sweet West Texas crude, only to repeat the ritual a gazillion times a day. Jack, our rancher friend, was getting richer by the moment. Even we felt rich. If I could have only gotten my numb, lifeless lips on that old horse head, I would have kissed it! Stumbling down the gravel road, we soon found our way back to the truck. The moon was out by then. The wind was still. Yes, the morrow would bring us fine bird hunting weather.

Jules and the Burro

Dangers in the field often present themselves in odd and unexpected ways. Generally our hunting dogs are more at risk than we are. Where we are cautious, they are generally not. We have had some close calls with rattlesnakes, cougars, bobcats, snares, poisons, porcupines, blizzards and bulls. Once I almost lost Jules to a very determined burro.

At the time we were hunting a new pasture, one that was heavily fenced and normally used for sheep production. Since coyotes are a real problem for ranchers here, the fences are substantial and well maintained. Usually their construction is a combination of barbed wire at the top with hog wire at the bottom. On this particular day I pitched Jules over the top strand of barbed wire and then climbed over after him. We hadn't gone a hundred feet when a large gray burro appeared from out of a little mesquite thicket. He was running directly at us, ears erect and pointed forward. I recall that at first Jules trotted out to meet him in a friendly greeting fashion but pulled up short. Realizing that diplomacy wasn't going to cut it this time, he turned tail and ran directly behind me. At twenty feet and still coming, the burro seemed extremely annoyed and big! This wasn't your ordinary "old prospector's donkey". He looked as big as a horse! Not knowing what else to do, I threw up my twenty gauge and fired the gun point-blank at an imaginary spot right between his ears but three feet high. Nothing! Not even a blink of those enormous round eyes. At the very last moment the burro nimbly sidestepped me and continued his relentless attack on Jules. It was the dog he was after, all right! Then I remembered what our rancher had once told us, "Don't ever allow your dogs near a burro here on the ranch. We keep burros here for one reason: to protect the sheep from the coyotes, and if you give 'em half a chance they'll kill your dogs just as quickly as they'll kill a coyote."

Jules was in a race for his life. He was now running in a wide circle with me at the center. He was going just fast enough to stay out in front of the burro while constantly keeping the irate beast in sight over his shoulder. It was as if Jules couldn't really believe what was happening to him. I could believe it! I was watching it: first, the burro would close the gap between them and with a quick sweeping motion throw out one of his front hooves in an attempt to trip the

dog. I knew only too well what would happen if Jules lost his footing. On the third pass the determined burro's hoof actually came in contact with Jules' hock and the dog very nearly went down. That was enough: the animal was about forty yards out when I shot him right square in the rump. He shuddered slightly, and then veered off into the little patch where he had come from. I knew that a light load of #8 shot at that range would have little lasting effect on the burro so I really wasn't too worried about him. Later that day I told our rancher about the incident and he looked down at Jules and said in utter amazement, "Jules Verne, I know of at least five flattened-out coyote carcasses in that pasture and they didn't die of old age. You are the proverbial lucky dog!"

Chapter 13
Jules Takes a Wife

Rhonda. It was probably the least appropriate name for a gun dog since — who knows — maybe, Jules Verne! Rhonda. That was her moniker. I still shake my head in dismay. Just form the letters for yourself, say "R-h-o-n-d-a," sounds like some kinda "hottie body" from the fifties, right? Go, Rhonda, go! Naturally, Jules loved her from the start.

Thornton came up with Rhonda when he heard I was matchmaking for Jules. Outside buying another female (I'd already tried that, unsuccessfully, with Spanky), borrowing a suitable female for breeding purposes wasn't going to be easy. I still recall Thornton's excitement:

"Hey, Fool! You're not gonna believe this but my hunting buddy over here has agreed to loan you his prized Brittany female so you can get some puppies. It took a lot of selling, but hey — Is that some good news or what?" Thornton crowed.

Secretly I was elated, but that's not the way Thornton and I worked.

"Not so fast, Thornton; you've gotta understand something. We're not talking about just any old dog here! We're talking about the mother of Jules' children!" I lectured unmercifully, "We are selecting a suitable queen for "The King"!

"Oh cripes, Rhonda is Bud's sister, you fool! She's got papers long as my leg, plus she's gorgeous. That guttersnipe of yours has absolutely no credentials, no pedigree whatsoever. Besides, Rocky said he's seen that same unmistakable little "monkey eyed" expression on every half-breed mutt outside Shreveport's city limits. You better thank me for this one."

"O.K., O.K, Thornton, you made your point!"

That weekend Gay and I met Thornton half way between Shreveport and Fort Worth. Grudgingly, I had to admit: Rhonda was everything Thorny had said. She was beautiful and truly a fitting queen for any king.

Rhonda fit in perfectly with our family. Besides being a fine looking dog, she had a calm, loving demeanor. Her coloring was liver and white; her coat, very shiny and wavy. Frankly her coat was a little curlier than the ideal, but I didn't care. She was from good hunting stock. That's what mattered. That and all those adorable little curls situated on top of her head.

Even Spanky took a liking to Rhonda and normally, Spanky greeted others of her kind with a low growl and a quick lip curl. Although it wasn't in the cards, I think Spanky would have made an excellent mother for Jules' pups. That was the original plan anyway, but apparently she had some sort of physiological problem that didn't allow her to have puppies. She certainly had a strong maternal instinct though. Spanky was primarily a kennel dog, but we used to bring her into the house fairly often so she could interact with the family. My girls, Emily and Marnie, loved to play with her. One of their games involved a family of stuffed animals the kids played with as children: a mother opossum with six babies. The girls delighted in feeding Spanky those fuzzy little gray opossum babies, one after the other. First, she'd take them very gently in her mouth and carry them off to a special little pile. Then she'd lie on her side and tenderly nestle her little marsupials and, pitiful as it may sound, try to coax them into nursing. Once she assumed that dreamy, contented maternal state of hers, any attempt to extract a baby elicited a violent snarl.

Our window of opportunity for puppies came two months later when Rhonda first showed signs of going into heat. I'd been preparing for this event and had their "bridal suite" all fixed up. Over the next day or two their union was consummated several times. It was Friday night as I recall, and as I fed and medicated my dogs before turning in, I thought to myself with some relief how smoothly their breeding campaign had gone. Everything was lovely. We had the King. We had the Queen. We even had a nursemaid. All we needed now were some puppies.

The next morning as I rounded the corner of the house, I made a shocking discovery. The kennel door to the bridal suite stood wide open! And where the night before frolicked The King and Queen... now resided thin air.

The search was on. I had lost dogs before and I knew that timing was critical but still, I didn't have much to go on. Had Jules and Rhonda made their escape sometime during the night or had they gotten out sometime early that morning? If at night, they could go undetected for hours. At night, even in the city, who would ever see them? And just how far could a pair of hunting dogs travel in eight or ten hours — and in which direction? The possibilities were endless; mind boggling! By far the evening escape scenario was the most alarming, so naturally, being the paranoid that I am, it was the one I gravitated most toward. I started canvassing the area immediately and so did Gay with the girls, but to no avail. Two long, frustrating days later we were no closer to finding the runaway pair than we were when we started.

A lot of things go through your mind in situations like this. For me, hard questions concerning responsibility and those inevitable feelings of gut-wrenching guilt topped the list. The biggie, of course: had I been so foolishly distracted by the prospect of "all those puppies" that somehow, I had failed to latch the gate properly? That concept still sounds pretty familiar. I must have asked myself that one thirty thousand times at least. Remember, too, that one of the dogs we were looking for was a female "in heat," which presented unimaginable, far-reaching problems, even if she was found! One thing was certain however: despite the fact that I dreaded calling a perfect stranger to tell him that I had lost his dog; the prospect that I'd never see Jules again was even more abhorrent and totally untenable.

Mid morning of the third day found me at the office. I'd been driving the southwest side of the city since first light and stopped in to see if there was any news. No news — everything that could be done had been done: the signs, the ads, the calls to the newspapers, and yeah, the calls to the pound — particularly those made on an hourly basis because I didn't trust them at all! The awful prospect of Jules and Rhonda being transported hundreds of miles across interstate lines also played constantly through my mind like an endless loop. Of course, the real danger in a situation like this has nothing to do with dognapping or apathetic public servants. The real danger is "tire poisoning," anybody knows that, but the prospect of seeing Jules or Rhonda lying on the side of the road was a brand of reality I didn't even want to think about.

By noon I was numbly driving south on Line Avenue, humming along to an old Chuck Barry tune. Somehow the lyrics fit... "Driving along in my automobile...with no particular place to go..." That was me: totally without a plan. And how was my state of mind? Well, I know I was desperate to the point of being delusional all-day Saturday and Sunday. I'm sure I was well beyond that by Monday. The higher power route had been

"German Shorthair in the Corn Flowers" 12x24

covered thoroughly within the first half-hour of discovering Jules' disappearance. Fervent prayer and all those countless mea culpas hadn't produced much, either. I don't believe I've ever felt quite so hopeless. I had to find my dog! It was then that I came up with the novel idea of giving mental telepathy a whirl! Mental Telepathy — now there's a sure sign of mental duress, you may wonder? Actually, given the strange incident I experienced growing up, the concept may not be all that far fetched, after all. Please, allow me to explain further –

As a boy, perhaps five or six years old, my father moved our family from our home in New Orleans, Louisiana to Fort Worth, Texas, where he had expanded his Import/Export business. After World War II there were no commercial mosquito repellants on the market so his business plan was to fill that void with army surplus "mosquito dope". The manufacturing facility, as I recall, was a pretty grim looking affair: an old dusty, gray building made of corrugated tin and located in downtown Fort Worth. I remember men off-loading railroad cars full of large wooden cases. These boxes were filled with little brown bottles that were emptied into a huge crusher. After being ground-up the oily, rank smelling, "medicine" was filtered of broken glass and then placed into attractive little *clear* bottles to be sold to the general public.

Anyway, I can't really remember much about that trip; I was only five years old at the time, and it was very late at night. To most people the prospect of driving through the night is not a pleasant one, but for my father it was preferable to day travel for several reasons (...having nothing to do with the marketing of suspicious *medicinal elixirs* prior to FDA approval, I promise!). Since he never required much sleep, driving all night allowed him to work or play the entire day through; really, a pretty logical use of time when you think about it. He also believed it far safer at night due to the fact that there were less people on the roads. It was certainly more comfortable, especially during the heat of summer, when night temperatures in the South are a lot more bearable. Anyway, we did a lot of traveling at night. Usually in a situation like this, my mother would prepare comfortable little pallets for my sister and me to sleep on — my sister on the back seat and me on the floor below her. The one thing I vividly remember about this particular journey though, was that somewhere along our route my father stopped at an all-night gas station. I remember waking up with a start and with the strangest sensation. It was the "realization" that the girl I would eventually fall in love with and marry was somewhere nearby, asleep. This is not the type of thought pattern I would attribute to a five year old child and certainly, not this child. But that is the hard, irrefutable concept that occurred to me that night under the glaring lights of an all-night service station. I remember sitting there in absolute wonderment, trying to visualize her face, the visage of the girl I would choose to spend a lifetime with — all the while, with my mother and sister sleeping there in the car beside me, and my father who I could see through the smudged windows of the station, sipped coffee and talking endlessly with the attendant inside. And that was it: the single, puzzling memory that has stayed with me always. In the years that followed, I would occasionally reel back that odd experience, always wondering: where is she right now and what is she doing?

Gay, to me, has always been an enigma. Beautiful far beyond "my words", somehow that minute detail never really connected with her. If she ever traded on her looks I'm seriously not aware of it. About the only personal acknowledgement of her physical attributes I can remember was when she laughingly confided that one of her classmates in the Art Department at Ole Miss had told her that her profile was exactly like the one he'd seen on a bar of soap.

The night I proposed to Gay while we were students at the University of Mississippi, I whispered in her ear: "I've always wondered who you were and where you were and I love you." The big question for me had been answered — the one I was most interested in at the time — I now knew *who* she was. It would be years later when I connected all the dots, tracing my family's route that fateful night, up north from New Orleans through the swamps and low country of South Louisiana to the fertile farm land and the piney woods of North Louisiana on Highway 1 to Shreveport where Gay lived as a child, only one block from the route we traveled. I was stunned at the realization and I immediately told Gay of my discovery. Since she was a big fan of the supernatural at the time, she was totally mesmerized. *Oooh, spooky!* So, was it Shreveport where I had my premonition? *Only the sighted one knows for sure —*

So aside from this single childhood episode where my union with Gay had been predetermined at age five, I had little experience with the *paranormal,* as they used to call it. Sure, I'd seen a few movies on the subject, mostly comedies, but the subject of mental telepathy and extrasensory perception were areas I knew very little about, so I was pretty skeptical. At any rate, due to the nature of my agitation, I would become a willing student. I didn't have an experienced "guide" leading me, so my technique may sound a little crude. But at least I had a general idea what was supposed to take place. I reasoned that loosening my death grip on the steering wheel just a little, would be an appropriate first step. I was tense. My over burdened psyche yearned for relaxation. I then began rotating, then rolling my head very slowly. That felt nice: sort of relaxing really, as long as I didn't get too close to the curb. Remember, I didn't have a guide so I had to improvise. The final phase required a mind meld with the party to be contacted — that, of course, being Jules. I engaged that part of my psyche. It seemed to work. Now what happened next, I'll grant you, sounds absolutely ridiculous but I don't know how else to tell it. It was as if the steering wheel wanted to turn in my hands at the next street. I

was no longer gripping a steering wheel at all. It was more like a divining rod. I completed the turn onto Elmwood as if by remote control. And it felt good! Finally, after two and a half days, I was getting somewhere. Maybe there was something to all this hocus-pocus, after all! Driving slowly down Elmwood, I came to Creswell. Here, there was no sensation whatsoever. So, I continued on. By the end of the next block the vibes were coming on strong again. And just as before, the divining rod in my hands took control and all of a sudden, I was driving south again, having turned onto Highland. Now I was gaining speed: past Ratcliff, past McCormick, past Slattery and Dudley until finally, I came to a stop at Ockley. I sat there a moment at the stop sign. The sensations I had been experiencing were definitely interesting, but far from conclusive. The hillside in front of me was alive with kids at play; recess at First Baptist Academy was a happy, carefree spot, all right. "Now this is more like it; Jules loves children. Surely this was the type of place for a lost dog," I thought. Scanning the opposing hillside, I witnessed hundreds of children doing what they do best: some were running, others skipping, laughing, chasing here, chasing there, climbing up, sliding down, lots of kids, lots of activity, but no Jules.

I sat there for an indeterminate span of time thinking, not yet dejected, mind you, but still not quite as elated as I had been just a few minutes before. I was mulling over my options when peripheral movement on my left side drew attention to a nondescript dog walking directly toward me on the sidewalk. As he drew closer, my first impression was that he was very small, very wet, and absolutely covered with mud. In a daze, I slowly opened the car door and the filthy little dog hopped inside, where it slipped under my legs and onto the seat beside me. With a sigh of relief, I was presented with a sweet kiss from a very tired Jules Verne.

Cynics will question my story, but I stand by it. I can't

explain it exactly. Nor have I ever been tempted to duplicate the experience. Maybe I'm just so happy with the outcome that I've never felt the need to explore it further. One thing sure: I've never been so "desperately motivated to try absolutely anything," since. And I'm thankful for that. Call it coincidence. Call it Providence. Call it a lie. The fact remains that I found my dog in just ten minutes after employing a strange resource we may all possess. Who knows? Incidentally, not long ago I told the Rock about my odd childhood experience involving Gay and our "predestined" relationship and marriage, fully expecting him to be filled with awe and amazement, but his response was a little more characteristic, "Why do you want to lie to her like that?" She's been with you for over thirty years. She's not going anywhere!"

The next morning, I got a call from an old family friend who said she'd read about our missing Brits in the local newspaper and believed that the dog had taken up residence on her back porch. I arrived at the Peg's house to find Rhonda and a new friend! Rhonda's acquaintance was a medium sized, shepherd type of the male persuasion, naturally. He seemed very attentive, relentless even, to the extent that he chased our car for several blocks until I lost him on a straightaway.

After arriving back at the house, I immediately called Dan Core, our veterinarian, for advice on what course to follow with Rhonda. True, I was tremendously happy to have Rhonda back but obviously, we were going to be faced with a paternity question issue at some point. Dan agreed. What followed I still find very interesting. He instructed me to immediately put the dogs back together and allow them to breed for as long as they would. And we did. The breeding continued for several more days. Dan's contention was that we would, more than likely, have what he called a "broken litter", meaning that there would be multiple fathers. In other words, some of the pups would be full bred Brittany spaniels (Rhonda + Jules Verne),

and others would have mixed breeding (Rhonda + ?). Generally, with a female dog, two eggs are dropped from the ovaries every twenty-four hours throughout the full term of the heat. We knew that Jules had bred Rhonda several times at the front of her cycle and several times at the end. What happened in between was anyone's guess.

That is, "anyone" but The Rock. Apparently he knew more about Rhonda's indiscretions than anyone else did. Almost immediately he began referring to Rhonda in disparaging terms (i.e....that slut...that trollop, etc.). Oh, how he railed! I tried to impress upon him the difference between human behavior and animal behavior, but he refused to have any of it. To this day, we still have heated discussions as to Rhonda's basic nature and sense of decorum.

With fingers crossed, Gay and I waited. Sixty-three days later Rhonda delivered her first pup: a beautiful, champagne and white colored male my daughter Emily named "Nemo." We were elated; Gay especially, since she had acted as midwife. Naturally we assumed that the pale lemon tint was Jules' own orange/red coloring in an early phase. Weeks later we would find this to be so. Puppy number two, born five minutes into the birthing process was champagne and white, just like number one. Puppies three and four were liver and white: Rhonda's mark. Everything was going extremely well; so well in fact, that I gave the Rock a call to fully apprise him of every aspect of the blessed event. I told him that we had four puppies, all apparently full blooded Brittany Spaniels. He could tell that I was pleased and his response was respectful, albeit measured. "And how is the mother?" he asked in a stilted tone. We had at this point something of a fragile truce going on. "Quite well, thank you." I cautiously responded. "She had her last puppy fifteen minutes ago. I don't suppose she's all done. Maybe four's all she's going to have?" That was all the Rock could handle. A torrent of sarcasm then rained down upon me, "Get real; she's gonna have at least a dozen pups! Why, that trollop hasn't even gotten to Line Avenue yet! And as for those colors, before it's over with you're gonna see every color of the rainbow; you wait!" Well, so much for the truce....

Thirteen pups later, Rhonda decided it was time to call a halt to the procession, the first phase of her mission completed. Gay and I marveled at the spectacle — all those puppies — each squalling and squirming for its position in the world, lined up along Rhonda's belly. It was truly impressive. And as if driven by the Rock's prophesy, we witnessed that night a plethora of colors, too. Perhaps not every single color of the rainbow (I don't recall any greens or blues), but certainly there was a lot of variety. By our calculation, and after careful analysis, the tally was: Jules = 7, Others = 6. Not a perfect score, by any means, but one I could live with.

In the weeks that followed we grew to love all our puppies, not just Jules Verne's prodigy, but the black and white ones and the brown ones, too. One thing became readily apparent to us all: the little off-brands were much larger and stronger than the Brits. But that really didn't matter much because Rhonda was a good mother and a good milk producer, too. At the dinner table everyone got his or her fair share. Jules, too, was a fine, patient parent. Normally, you don't associate the father of the litter as taking a very active role in such things but Jules was different. Once, he jumped from a second floor balcony out into the back yard in order to be with his puppies and me. There were a few tense minutes there when frankly, I didn't know if Jules was going to survive the fall. But eventually he staggered up and with some effort got his wind back, apparently no worse for wear.

In the end we'd find homes for all the big, husky cousins. And as for the Brittany Spaniels: well naturally, I gave Thorny the pick of the litter. He deserved that special deference and because he's a good judge of dogs, he chose Pops, the fattest,

the finest, and most aggressive of all the pups and secretly, my favorite. Pops had a curious little cowlick that ran the length of his nose and ended between his eyes, very much like the ridge found on the back of a Rhodesian Ridgeback (How about that, I've wondered the same thing!). To Rhonda's owner we gave a beautiful liver and white female. And as for little Nemo, namesake of the dashing captain of the *Nautilus* in "Twenty Thousand Leagues under the Sea," he went to a good friend, as did Jennie, another liver and white female. We decided to keep Laddie Buck and Willie (the runt), and of course, Precious Lamb.

A month or so later we'd be called upon to give up "the Lamb" to a friend whose family had suffered a terrible loss. It seemed that while on a walk with his wife, my friend's Brittany had stepped out into the street and was killed by a car. With tears running down his cheeks, Howard told us how his wife was so devastated by the event that she refused to leave her bedroom. To further complicate matters, it was Easter weekend and their children were expected home from college at any moment. Howard felt that if only he had a Brittany puppy waiting for them when they arrived home, the news of their beloved pet's death would not be quite so traumatic for them. What else could we do?

It's been almost sixteen years since those special warm spring days with the pups, when my backyard resembled the surface of the moon, with holes everywhere and hardly a single flower or blade of grass remaining. And when late in the afternoon I'd arrive home from work, I'd head for the gate and give a whistle and there'd be puppy heads popping up all over the place, like so many little marmots. Then there would be Jules, standing there happy as could be, surrounded by all his kin in the warm afternoon sunlight. Yes, he was a sight to see.

"West Texas Racehorse" 16x20

Chapter 14
The Road Home

I had a client once who told me that as a boy his father would routinely drag him along with him quail hunting on weekends. It seems that the father had a string of bird dogs that he cherished a great deal. According to the client, his father loved those dogs almost as much as him. Clearly the man wanted to share with his son this important aspect of his life, probably hoping that the boy would ultimately take up the sport on his own and in time perhaps, have it become as meaningful to him as it had been to the father. Beautiful mental images of a young boy and his dad enjoying special moments afield played through my head as he spoke. I had enjoyed special times like these with my father; today I enjoy reliving them. The client then proceeded to tell me that he hated those Saturday afternoon romps with his dad and that frankly, if given a choice, he would have just as soon shot his father's dogs as the quail they were supposed to be hunting. It was all pretty much the same to him.

We are what we are. I am a hunter. I make no excuse for that. Obviously my client was not (I still don't know exactly what in the hell he was!). And although the taking of life is integral to the type of hunting that I'm most acquainted with, it is still my least favorite aspect of it. Killing game humanely for the table is a solemn responsibility that ethical hunters accept. As long as I eat what I kill, I can justify it — if indeed, it needs justification. It's just that simple for me. At least it is for now.

So it was this endeavor that drew us together: the age-old ritual of hunting; a small group of us traveling west toward Big Spring, looking forward to a landmark weekend of gloriously exhilarating dog work and heart thumping quail shooting. With me this trip were Jules' sons, Laddy Buck and Willie. It was opening weekend and they were rip-roaring and ready to go, on their first ever hunt for wild birds. No other two dogs were any more prepared for the challenge than they were.

As we drove past Fort Worth the sun was hanging low on the horizon. It was at that special time of the day when the fields and the trees and the ponds all turn golden. Maybe it's the air that turns to gold, I can't say; anyway, it's special. Through half closed eyes I stared at the rolling caramelized landscape and thought about Jules; thought about the good times we had shared — and the bad, and particularly the period we were concluding. Aside from the pups and all the wonderful and exciting moments associated with them, it had not been a particularly good year, especially where Jules was concerned.

It was getting colder outside. I hoped that Jules was warm at home. This was the first time I'd ever left him behind. But then I really didn't have much choice about that, did I? The cough would end it for him; the cough would rob me of my friend. Slowly it came over him in the spring, a persistent hacking that Dan quickly diagnosed as congestive heart failure. Dan was good. He always got it right. But then sometimes, the truth is the last thing you want to hear. In this case it was the defining moment when I knew my days with Jules on this earth were numbered.

Although we had treated Jules for heartworms years before when he first came to us, it was later, perhaps four or five years later, that he was diagnosed a second time with the same malady. Dan would theorize that the first treatment, performed by another veterinarian in a time when the regimen was still unperfected, had been ineffective in ridding him of the disease. So my little buddy would be required to undergo the same hazardous treatment a second time. Sadly, by then the damage had already been done.

Like a gloating parent at his kid's first football game, I studied Jules' fine little pups. To my way of thinking they were

"The Boys" 24x36

quite handsome. Sitting there shoulder to shoulder in their travel kennel, I thought to myself that I could see a bit of Jules in each of them. In Laddy it was readily apparent since he and his father shared the same red and white coat. With Willie the resemblance was less marked, since his coloring was that of his mother: liver and white. All the same, he had the look. Both demonstrated Jules' distinctive ticking, mostly on their legs, an unmistakable Jules hallmark. I couldn't help but smile when I thought back maybe seven or eight years to a time when Jules was himself, a young dog, new to our family and friends. Curious about Jules' conformation and probably his pedigree, Gay had an old childhood chum over to check him out. The girl raised Golden Retrievers and supposedly knew dogs. Gay, of course, was eager for her opinion. Upon seeing Jules, the girl sniffed disdainfully and said with little reservation, "I don't know, Gay... he's so scrawny and... ooh, what's that all over his legs? Is he dirty?" That "eye of the beholder" thing, it's an elusive, subjective animal, I guess.

Just outside Palo Pinto, our troop came upon a familiar, festive looking joint called the "Snake Farm". We had passed its signs and garishly painted buildings dozens of times over the years, but it had never raised much interest with us. Normally we see far more snakes in the field than we care to encounter. This time, however, was different. The Burma-shave style signage along the interstate featured nasty-looking, no-shouldered critters of all description and it gave me an idea. I had just read an article in *Gun Dog Magazine* on how the author had "snake proofed" his hunting dogs. For us, this would be an invaluable service since poisonous snakes are always a threat, particularly in the early season. Rattlesnakes, Cottonmouths and Copperheads all exist where we hunt, and unfortunately for our hunting companions, the majority of our dogs show little fear of these deadly, cold blooded creatures.

According to the article, the snake proofing procedure was fairly simple to implement provided you have two important ingredients: an electronic collar and a defanged rattlesnake. The electronic collar is standard operating equipment for a lot of people who train bird dogs. We had several of those. The defanged rattlesnake was another matter.

After discussing our plan with the "Snake Farm" proprietor (a pretty knowledgeable guy), we found out that although he had hundreds of fully equipped rattlers on hand, he didn't have a single "defanged rattler" for our project. He recommended that we use a bull snake instead and, "lucky for us," he did have one of those: a big, ill-tempered six footer. Our snake expert reasoned that a harmless bull snake would work just as well as a rattlesnake, since the two snakes look and act almost identically. Plus, as he pointed out, they're a heck of a lot safer to deal with than rattlesnakes. Incidentally, we couldn't help but notice that he was right on concerning the two snakes' striking similarities. The beautiful diamondback pattern worn by the bull snake was, in fact, almost identical to that of the rattlers' and, amazingly, the bull snake shook its tail convincingly and somehow imitated that unmistakable rattling sound we associate with its deadly cousin. Clearly, Mother Nature has provided the lowly bull snake with its "Bad to the Bone" facade as a protective device. Predators further up the food chain would certainly give an irate bull snake wide birth, particularly if they had any experience with poisonous snakes. I know this one would, anyway.

One by one our hunting dogs were subjected to the bull snake. It was interesting how some of the dogs took the bait immediately, many of them older, more experienced dogs. Invariably they would cautiously stalk the serpent: tail wagging, circling, curious — slowly — ever so slowly — getting closer and closer to the coiled reptile, until finally, nose to nose with the bristling, rattling snake, they'd get a little too close. And for their trouble, a lightening response would ensue. With awesome speed and raging aggression, the bull snake would strike and at that very moment, we, too, would strike, not with tooth or fang, or anger, but with cool, detached calculation. A little thumb pressure at the right moment on a small black button was all that was needed. The electronic collar would do the rest.

Some question the use of the electronic collar as an ethical training aid, particularly where "man's best friend" is concerned. I did. For years I resisted using a "collar" on the dogs I worked with. Somehow I never could square its use. But in the end, the efficiency of it and more importantly, the humanity of the device eventually won out. There are worse things than mild electrical shock. How many fine hunting dogs have been beaten unmercifully, or even shot at distance in the name of training? I've been there. I've seen the "old timers" at work. I know now that my earlier resistance to the use of a remote trainer was ruled largely by ignorance and I admit an over-sensitive concern for the dog and his feelings. Sadly, any training device or technique can be misused. It's up to us to make sure that it's not. I've read that a dog's intelligence is comparable to that of a two-year old human. I can believe that. I can also believe that young dogs have a natural tendency to give up everything they've learned once they're off their leash and running free. Anger, frustration, and eventually desperation have driven many good men to resort to cruel and arcane training techniques. And there's no need for it. We read endless accounts of beautifully trained gun dogs performing incredible feats of wonder in our favorite outdoor books and magazines. Well, rare is the dog that arrives at that station in his life without some sort of conflict with his trainer. An appropriate correctional jolt judiciously and conservatively applied, is harmless and can accomplish wonders while relieving both dog and trainer a lot of stress.

And as ultimate proof of the electronic collar's worth: twelve thoroughly conditioned, "snake proofed" bird dogs rested outside in our dog trailer, ready for the field, and more than likely, safe from any future snake-bite. Actually, for some reason,

my two Brittany pups didn't need any reinforcement at all. Call it good parenting if you like, but they wouldn't go anywhere near that snake. Instead they hung up twenty feet out and barked their heads off. Can you believe, one of the guys made the rude accusation that I was covering my eyes during their test. They were probably just keying off my anxiety.

It was late when we arrived at the ranch. A message was waiting for me there to call home — not a good sign. Gay picked up the phone on the first ring; another oddity, since she always waits until at least the third ring. She sounded shaken, having just gotten back from Dan Core's clinic. Apparently Jules had taken a turn for the worst shortly after we'd left that afternoon. He was on oxygen and according to Gay, Dan had very serious doubts as to his survival. He assured Gay that he would remain with Jules whatever the outcome.

Jules had been on heavy doses of Digitalis for months. Still he heaved and coughed as his brave little heart attempted to throw off the drowning fluid buildup. It was pitiful to watch, exhausting for him, exhausting for us. Everyone in our family looked on in helplessness, not knowing quite what to do. In retrospect I don't believe euthanasia was ever considered. But clearly, for dog or man, this was no way to live. I knew that. I knew what was coming. But sometimes, for some people, life and death concepts are difficult to confront in real terms. I thought I was prepared for the obvious, the inevitable. And I wasn't. It was after midnight when Gay called again. This time, her message left no room for hope or further rationalization. Jules was gone.

In times of emotional stress we all seek relief in some form or another. Even animals are known to grieve the passing of their own and they are without human intelligence or souls. Or at least that's what we're told. Crow hunting as a sport is widely justified as a form of varmint control. As such, the hunter need not feel obligated to eat what he shoots. Convenient how that

"Vizslas" 32x48

"Willie" 16x20

works. But it was not the wanton waste that permanently cured me from hunting crows. No, you see, one afternoon while pursuing them we tarried a little too long at our last set up. The ground, as I recall, was strewn with lifeless black carcasses, shot and left for the varmints to clean up. After a while, we began to notice that crows, one by one, were returning to that spot. But not as before — not dipping and diving in search of the fake owl — their angry caws merging with our own duplicitous, angry calls. No; one by one, they quietly came in on black velvet wings and perched high in the pine trees over their fallen brothers to mourn them with the saddest of song.

I understand now that the mourning ritual is common with crows. During the grieving process we as human beings follow similar patterns or rituals in our search for peace and closure. Many of us are comforted by our acceptance of a higher power, through prayer and a fervent belief in an afterlife. Is it our ability to believe in the hereafter that allows us to come to terms with personal loss?

The night Jules died sleep was out of the question. I stood for hours out back, behind the little ranch house, near the corral, looking up into the heavens, marveling at the stars, the planets and thinking about a little dog who'd come into our lives years before, the little dog no one seemed to want, not even me. Unquestionably, Jules had filled an important void in my life. I had little experience with human loss; I was lucky in that way. I had lost my father years before, so naturally I thought about him, too, that night. But that wasn't anything out of the ordinary. What was unusual though, and absolutely startling to me was that I began thinking of her.

She would be sixteen years old had she lived. She doesn't have a name. She was the stillborn daughter whose life was never realized, never appreciated — my daughter. Call it non-reality or some type of mind-numbing detachment, but I had never really thought about her as a human being — never dared place a face on her — never even wondered how or where she was! Was that the height of self-absorbed insensitivity or had I been in some kind of escape based stupor all those years? I hope to God that it was psychologically necessary, but why?

What age will she be when at last we do meet? I wonder. Will she resemble Emily, her twin sister, the daughter who received our love? Will she have long dark hair, or will she be blonde like her mother? Will the twins share a common, sardonic wit? I have no idea of these things, but I do know this: she will be lovely, I am sure. Her mother doesn't know I think these thoughts. We have never spoken of her in these terms. How will Gay react when she reads these words?

That night I found solace thinking about a daughter I had never known, dreaming of a final reunion where she, her mother, her sisters and I will at last meet, realizing and accepting once and for all, the importance of family, knowing in my heart that ultimately nothing, not even the cradling arms of the Great Outdoors can compare to the great unwavering love we share. What a wonderful meeting that will be. Frankly, I've never felt such peace before or since. And today, almost twenty years later when late at night I think of her, somehow, the daunting prospect of my own mortality becomes a little less frightening and somehow more acceptable, at times, even preferable. Is that the answer then, when we come to really understand that there is nothing to fear on the other side; that life in the hereafter will be a thousand times better there than anything we will ever experience here? I had heard the words all my life but their meaning had eluded me. My epiphany — what millions before me have come to understand, finally, I think I began to understand. I look forward to that day when we will all be together. And surely if there's a place in heaven for one little girl, then maybe there's room enough for a small dog, too; a hidden valley where we can all reunite as a family.

This image is available as a signed, limited edition print: www.waynesimmonsart.com

 AINBOW BRIDGE

"According to legend there is a place just this side of heaven called the Rainbow Bridge. Supposedly, when an animal dies that has been especially close to someone here on earth, that animal goes to the Rainbow Bridge. There he finds beautiful hills, streams and meadows and friends to run and play with. There's plenty of food and water and sunshine, and every one of these special creatures is warm and comfortable. All the animals that were old and infirm here on earth are restored to their original health and vigor. And those who were hurt or maimed are made whole and strong again, just as we remember them in our dreams of days gone by. All these animals are happy and content, except for one small thing — they each miss someone very special to them whom they had to leave behind. They run and play together until that special day comes when one suddenly stops and looks into the distance. His bright eyes are intent. His eager body begins to quiver. Suddenly he begins to run from the group, flying over green grass, his legs carrying him faster and faster. You have been spotted, and when you and your special friend meet, you cling together in joyous reunion, never to part again. The happy kisses rain upon your face, your hands again caress the beloved head and you look once more into the trusting eyes of your friend, so long gone from your life but never absent from your heart. Then together, you and your special friend cross the Rainbow Bridge."

- Author Unknown

It was beginning to get light in the East, the sky taking on that faint, rosy pale of morning. Songbirds rustled overhead in the stunted live oaks that surrounded the barnyard, their morning song performed as a spirited tribute to another glorious day here on earth. And in the distant mesquite, the soft, plaintive three-syllable call of a lost bobwhite quail could be heard. And in response, a series of three, three-syllable whistles, almost inaudible peeps, really. "Come back, come back to the safety of the circle," the anxious family member seems to whisper. Straying far from the protection of the covey is a risky proposition for all concerned. Life can be tenuous here. Hungry cats and coyotes hang in the shadows waiting to hear their furtive calls, always ready to hone in on a now vulnerable family group. And, as if by providential decree, one within the covey will inevitably break silence, ignoring impending danger, and emit the soft comeback call. "Come back, come back to the protection of the circle," he whispers. It was time for the long road home.

Shreveport, Louisiana, twelve hours later...

The girl from Dan's office refused to look at me as she handed me the small bundle. It was Jules. He was wrapped in an old blue blanket that I recognized. He seemed very small indeed, as I laid him on the car seat next to me. You're expected to feel terrible loss at the passing of a loved one: a human friend, a human blood relative. Are we supposed to feel guilt when we take the death of a non-human friend just as hard?

When I returned home with Jules I went out to the kennel area where I had already dug the hole. Gay was standing there under the old pecan trees. Jules' boys lined up along the chain link fencing. Their expressions were quizzical yet, at the same time, very sad, very somber. Although they had never experienced the death of one of their own, I do believe they knew what was going on and that their hearts were breaking just like ours. I turned to Gay and, with some difficulty, thanked her for bringing Jules home to me from the barn that day so many years before. Then, with his sons looking on, I buried my dog.

Years later I still think of Jules. I remember tramping through endless golden fields, the earthy smells, the moving sage grass, the wind, the sky, the birds — and, best of all, a small red and white dog running toward me. He is bringing me a gift.

The End

Epilogue

Shreveport, Louisiana, Twenty years later...

I hadn't seen the Rock in a while so I dropped by his office the other day. He was propped up behind that big mahogany desk of his, those little cheaters he wears, crowding the end of his nose. Stuff was piled up everywhere, mostly old hunting and fishing photos and magazines and, of course, lots of catalogs — a sure sign that hunting season was somewhere nearby.

"I thought I'd buy a couple of dozen of these..." he said, his eyeballs glued on something that elicited a strange, trance-like stare. The stubby little finger pointed down to a photo of some high priced mallard field decoys in one of the catalogs. "Yeah, these will look good down at the swag. You know, like real ducks walking up out of the water and into that little wheat field Uncle Tom planted for us." Obviously the Rock was taking a mental break from his "filling and billing" gig.

"Star, stop that whining!" he screamed hysterically. "She starts that whining every time you come in the door!" His consternation was building to a crescendo; too much pressure wading through all those catalogs, I guessed. "Her hearing must be incredible, and all that high pitched whining just kills my ears." Star is the Rock's three year old Yellow Lab and she is very fond of me. She likes him, too — just a whole lot better.

"Rock, I don't see my manuscript up here on your desk, anywhere. You must be finished with it." I had hand delivered the first draft of Jules' story to his office several weeks earlier and I was curious as to his take on my handiwork.

Immediately, the Rock assumed the position. "Yes, I can see you're a little apprehensive... hehh, hehh, hehh. Perhaps, you're thinking that the Rock has taken offense at something you've written? Perhaps, he's even a little miffed with the author?"

"Not exactly, but what *did you* think? Thornton says I need to rename it, "The King and I". He said you'd understand."

"Oh, how clever of Thornton! Frankly, I haven't had time to finish that fictional account of yours. I've been far too busy with a project of my own — interviewing lawyers for a character assassination suit I'm considering." And by the way, I'm going to make far more money off that totally fabricated story of yours than you ever dreamed of!" Pitter, patter, pitter, patter, I could hear Star slipping down the hall. She was coming to visit me.

So some things never really change, but with time others do. Obviously, the Rock hasn't changed a great deal. But my girls are hardly the children they once were. They're grown now, living in distant cities with their own sweet families. Gay and I still live in the same Louisiana city where we always lived; in the very same corner house we shared with Jules, as a matter of fact. We spend a lot more of our time up in Wisconsin now. Years ago we bought a little farm in Door County near a quiet little village named Ellison Bay. We have a studio/gallery right there on the place where I paint and display my art. This is something I always wanted to do, so in that respect I am very thankful.

Today my kennels stand empty. Rarely ever do I venture back there anymore. I guess the overturned water buckets and the dusty food bowls are an unpleasant reminder of another time. Of course, Jules is gone now but the memories linger. It's been many, many years since last I felt that soft sweet head come quietly under my hand. And then with that quick upward bounce, experience that all too familiar wakeful jolt, as cold wet nose and muzzle come slamming up into my palm, prodding.

As went Jules so, too, went Spanky, then Rhonda and much later, the boys and a few other notables I failed to mention who enriched my life along the way. I haven't been bird hunting in several years now. I get the occasional invitation still, but somehow I always seem to find some excuse as to why I can't fit it into my schedule. As any real bird hunter knows, running your own dogs is ninety percent of the thing, anyway.

Recently I've been toying with the idea of getting another dog or two, or maybe three. As I tell Gay, it's hard to stop at just one. The Rock and I toss that ball around quite a lot. I guess what I really need now is the right anchor dog. I've been offered a few fine-looking pups here lately, some with papers! But so far, the magic hasn't been there.

Sometimes as I drive out into the country, I find myself looking up ahead to the shoulder of the road and out into open fields, and off to the side, down shaded country lanes and paths. For some reason, an out-of-place splash of red or orange always seems to attract my attention. Definitely, the pound holds new fascination for me. Something will show up. After all, if there's any truth at all in the old adage, "Every bird hunter gets one outstanding bird dog in his lifetime"; then doesn't it seem reasonable, that for the hunter who really applies himself, *there may be two?*

Wayne Simmons has been an artist most of his life. Sporting Art, portraits of people, people and their pets, wildlife and landscapes all have their place in his art, but it's his dogs and their antics afield that offer recurring themes throughout his work. Wayne and his wife, Gay, divide their time between their homes in Shreveport, Louisiana and Door County, Wisconsin where the artist operates Simmons Studio/Gallery at 1375 County Road ZZ near Ellison Bay. His email address is wsimmonsad@aol.com, or you can visit his website: www.waynesimmonsart.com.

"I had rather see the portrait
of a dog that I know than
all the allegorical paintings
they can show me in the world."

Dr. Samuel Johnson. 1787

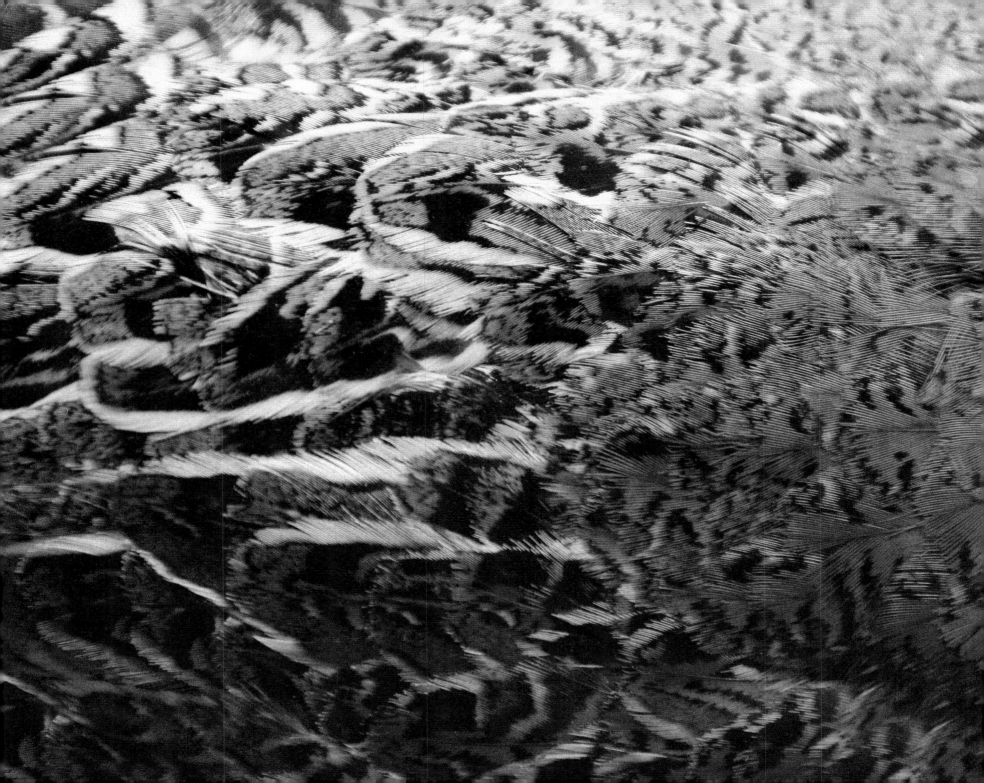